Living on the Edge

Coming of Age During Difficult Times

by

Ron Nicolas

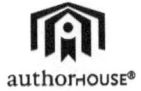

authorHOUSE®

AuthorHouse™
1663 Liberty Drive
Bloomington, IN 47403
www.authorhouse.com
Phone: 1-800-839-8640

First published by AuthorHouse 6/1/2009

Printed in the United States of America
Bloomington, Indiana
This book is printed on acid-free paper.

ISBN: 978-1-4389-7824-6 (sc)

Chapter Headings

Dedication

I owe a deep debt of gratitude to my departed parents whose care, discipline, devotion and hard work have enabled me to be the person I have become today. In their honor, I would like to dedicate the following poem.

I do not think of you lying in the wet clay
Of a lonely graveyard, I see
You walking down a lane among the poplars
On your way to the store, or happily
Going to Mass on a summer Sunday –
You meet us and say:
'Don't forget to see about the cattle-'
Among your earliest words the angels stray.
And I think of you walking hand in hand
Along a headland of green oats in June,
So full of repose, so rich with life…
O you are not lying in the wet clay,
For it is harvest time now and we
Are piling up the ricks against the moonlight
And you smile up at us – eternally.

Adapted from Patrick Kavanagh

Preface

This is a true story. It is one which I felt needed to be told before, like so many others, it was relegated to that eternal dustbin of history where untold stories go to die lonely deaths. While it is not world-shattering, I hope, nevertheless, that this small addition to the combined stories of the world will contribute to our understanding of what makes us the people we are. As well, it is not, in the true sense of the word, a story per se with its twists, plots, climax, drama and suspense. Essentially, by preference, I am more of a chronicler of tales than a raconteur or a spinner of yarns – as storytellers are often portrayed - as I feel stories try to amuse, titillate and entertain the reader rather than depict accurately and honestly the real events on the ground, as it were, - which is my sole intention here.

I had wanted to complete this book a few years ago shortly after the completion of my first novel entitled "Northern Lights – A Wilderness Adventure" published in 2005. Unfortunately, being the great procrastinator that I have always been, I kept putting it off for one reason or another. So now here goes. This book is dedicated to my parents, especially to my dear departed mother who passed away of cancer when I was only nineteen years old. I had hoped, at least, to complete this book for my dad, whose health was quickly deteriorating so he could either read it at his own leisure or have it read to him. It would have undoubtedly brought back vivid memories of our family life on the farm. Unfortunately, he succumbed to ill-health and passed away a few years ago. To make matters worse, a short time ago, I, too, was stricken with a form of cancer for which I have since been undergoing blood transfusions and several episodes of chemotherapy. This made me realize that if I did not get on with the task and complete this book soon, it might never get completed before, I, too, went to the great beyond and my own children would also miss out on an important chapter of my life.

A famous author by the name of Charles Dickens once wrote at the beginning of his classic novel 'A Tale of Two Cities' the following words: It was the best of times, it was the worst of times... Ever since I read these lines in grade school, I had always pondered at the gravity of these words. Try as much as I could I was never able to find words so rich, so encapsulating or so representative of every individual who ever lived and will ever live on this planet of ours. Everyone, from the poorest to the richest among us experiences great moments of joy and ecstasy - hence the best of times - and depressing or even deplorable moments - hence the worst of times. As quaint as this may sound, it is impossible to get away from this fact. In the same manner, life on our family farm was certainly a mixture of both. As the title of this book suggests, there were moments when it was doubtful whether life was really worth it. At other times, especially during the family get-togethers such as berry-picking, family softball tournaments with the neighbors – or as a family group, football in the front yard, horseback riding, sleighing in the winter and other such activities, these would raise our spirits and make us forget, temporarily at least, our everyday trials and tribulations and even make it appear that we were on top of the world, delusional as this may have been at the time.

This book is not merely about me, my family or life on our farm. It is that and much, much more. Primarily, it is really meant to appeal to a broader audience of people who have lived through similar times. In fact, it is also a sort of socio-historical expose, if you will, of these times as they were experienced then by countless families. As well, I have also included my thoughts about living conditions in the world at large, past and present, which seemed a propos here. It is my contention that many people, after reading this book, will be able to identify and relate to the way of life I have attempted to portray in the following pages.

William Shakespeare once remarked in one of his many tragedies that all the world is a stage and every man a player, in other words, everyone has a story to tell. Well, for better or for worse, here is mine. And it is my sincere hope that it will inspire others as well to do the same – as I am sure the Bard would have wanted it. It can be a truly rich, edifying and rewarding experience not just for them but also for their families and countless other readers who think that maybe they too can do that. And, of course, who knows, such so-called oral histories, when taken in combination with what historians, perhaps a bit flippantly, prefer to call 'real history', may even someday be invaluable sources of information for researchers of the future. Imagine, your life story could one day be a possible area of research and find itself in history books - a grandiose wish, I know. But one can only dream.

Chapter 1 – Introduction - The stage is set

Be strong
We are not here to play, to dream, to drift
We have hard work to do, and loads to lift
Shun not the struggle – face it, 'tis God's gift
Malthie Davenport Babcock[c]

I was born on June 16, 1948 – the third child of a family of seven siblings - in a small Midwestern town in the Canadian Province of Manitoba on the eastern edge of the Great Western Plains of Western Canada. It is a place where vast tracts of virgin boreal forests and gently rolling prairies come together to create an immense panoramic landscape of intertwining rivers bordered by giant oaks, aspens and poplars, as well as several varieties of cone-bearing pines, spruces and tamaracks all surrounded by rugged, often rocky, terrain. Several years before, my parents, then an eager young couple full of hopes and expectations for their future, had left my father's ancestral home further west, the result, I was told, of some minor disagreements with his own father, which have never been entirely revealed to me, and headed eastward to seek out their fortune. Unfortunately, much to their later chagrin and disparagement, the land they would finally settle on would prove to be largely unsuitable to grow much of anything of any value except, it seemed, for a variety of hardy weeds which would thrive anywhere and, when left unchecked, even prevail as the dominant species of grass.

As most of the arable land on the Prairies had already been used up, it had become the practice at the time, encouraged, no less, by a seemingly uncaring government intent on opening up the West to settlement at any cost, to try to acquire more agricultural land by pushing the frontiers of farm land ever deeper into the forbidding forest regions. It didn't seem to matter that most of this land was unsuitable for agriculture with the primitive technology of the time. More often than not this expansion into bush country would be at the expense of the hapless landowners as the land was gradually becoming less and less fertile with the gradual disappearance of an ever-decreasing layer of much needed topsoil the further east you went, thus necessitating an ever growing amount of back-breaking labor just to make the land marginally productive. Trees, boulders, and stumps, now becoming more prevalent as you moved further into the forest regions, as well as countless varieties of nettles, vetches and other weeds, had to be laboriously and painstakingly removed and burnt before any planting could ever be attempted. Oftentimes, it was even deemed necessary to plant among the trees themselves if one wanted some semblance of a crop to prevent the onset of starvation in such an unforgiving land. And, with the primitive tools and technology of the day, even then, it was often a futile and fruitless endeavor eventually forcing many a frustrated and discouraged farmer to simply abandon such menial and seemingly unrewarding work for the prospects, however bleak, of easier living elsewhere.

Nonetheless that was where my parents had decided to settle and that was where, come hell or high water, as my father had so prophetically stated, he was determined not only to make a go of it but also to exceed his own father's lifestyle even at the risk of later exposing his entire family to conditions which, over the years, would too often test the resolve of each and every one of us, as well as his own. His dream was to become one of the most successful homesteaders in the new land he was heading to. And, although he never stated it out loud, he would not relent until his goal had been achieved - or he was well on his way to achieving it.

In fact, he was single-mindedly determined and intent on making this land productive at all costs, and, as well, he was prepared to pay the price with his very life, if need be, for the sake of his family. That was the kind of man he was, stubborn but in a well-meaning way, a man who, in spite of his diminutive stature, would not hesitate to give of himself wholeheartedly in the pursuit of a goal he believed in. The land had always been part of him and that was all he knew. He could no more abandon it than a fish could leave the relative safety of the waters it swam in.

Eventually, though, and much too soon, disaster would rear its ugly head and cast a pall of sorrow on all his endeavors devastating him – and us - in the process. As a result of years of constant and continuous hard labor combined with a losing battle with cancer, my mom would be the first one to go as she succumbed to a slow and agonizingly painful death with her last dying thoughts being for the welfare of the family she was so unwillingly leaving behind to fend for itself. In the end, as well, after finally reluctantly leaving the farm behind, my father also would later pass away, a poor, disheartened and heart-broken man, never having achieved his ultimate goal of acquiring even moderate wealth to leave to his now grown-up children. It was, however, a tribute to my parents' resourcefulness and unbending will and determination in the face of such unrelenting adversity that the family endured and, in the end, succeeded in casting away the fetters of poverty which had, as far back as we could remember, always been our constant and steadfast loyal companions, with each one of us eventually becoming relatively successful and prosperous in his own right.

For that to become a reality, however, we had to leave and forsake the very land which had spawned us. It was either that or, like our parents slowly succumb to the unpredictable vicissitudes of this vast uncompromising desolation of sand, rocks and weeds. Truly, this had to be the land that God had given to Cain before casting him off alone in the wilderness to fend for himself. It is not to say, however, that there were not moments of great joys and contentment. But these were few and far in between as the greater part of our efforts was directed toward the unending toil of merely trying to keep the family together. And, luckily for the sake of our family, we never faltered but bravely, perhaps, a bit naively, and courageously struggled against all odds. I often wonder, though, how different life would have been for us if dad had chosen another profession besides farming in such an inhospitable and uninviting land. Was he guilty of bad judgment – a product of unbending pride combined with an attempt to show that he could make it on his own? Or was he simply innocently and unquestioningly following the advice of those who had, perhaps even callously, encouraged him to embark on that path – a path which could only lead to self-destruction in the end.

The world had, not so long ago, just gone through the turbulence of a period known as the Great Depression, often referred to, by some, as the dirty thirties, only to be followed by an unfathomable carnage, on the world scene, the proportions of which had never been witnessed before or since, and which, hopefully, we will never encounter again, where millions upon millions were displaced and lost their livelihoods and where countless more paid dearly with their very own lives. It was a time which would forever go down in history as a period of infamy.

And all along, as if the world had not suffered enough, that inseparable trio of poverty, misery and hunger had been nipping incessantly at their heels, keeping a close eye on everyone, as if attempting to break their collective will to survive or perhaps simply trying to keep their talons clutching firmly for as long as possible as if somehow sensing that their time of reckoning would eventually arrive. Slowly, perhaps unfortunately goaded by these tragic series of events unraveling on the world stage, people gradually did come together, one step at a time, as never before, in an attempt to break these iron shackles which had oppressed them and hindered their progress toward a brighter future. And with that unity came a renewed spirit of strength and vitality which created a common bond born out of the very pits of depression and shared experiences.

My own story really begins toward the end of this turmoil – a period which also witnessed great upheavals not only on the world stage but also in the meager and destitute lifestyles of individuals. It was a time when gaunt bodies and confused minds were slowly being rejuvenated by a renewed sense of optimism for the future – a sort of recognition at last, if you will, that what lay ahead had to be better than what was left behind. Unfortunately, as with every great upheaval, that sense of optimism, indeed reality itself, would take a long time to impress itself and permeate the whole fabric of society as many, including my own family, were left – some would even say abandoned – to forage and subsist on what little an unmerciful land would produce until, alas, we too, along with many others, would finally emerge and manage to break free of these vise-like constricting bonds and take our rightful place among the movers of the world and, in the process, to discretely and perhaps even contemptuously sneer at that past – a past which had unremorsefully held us hostage for so long, or so it certainly seemed at the time. And herein lay our dilemma – to boldly bury that past in the sands of time or praise it as a nostalgic part of our heritage. That was a decision each one of us had to make for himself.

Chapter 2 – A New Beginning

Amidst all this mayhem, just as the conflagration was erupting in Europe and the flames of war, famine and pestilence were gradually fanning themselves out in all directions to engulf an entire planet in their mortal grasp, my eldest brother unceremoniously came to this world on August 28, 1939 with the services of a midwife in Otterburne where my Dad and his Dad before him had also been similarly born and raised. Rarely could people afford to go to hospitals then which, in most cases, tended to be too far to travel to anyway. So, expectant mothers would often use the services of midwives – older women who were generally close family friends or relatives. In fact, most babies in these pioneer communities were often delivered by midwives as there were few available trained medical doctors then. As a footnote, I would also like to point out that as recently as the late 1960's when I was teaching in Northern Manitoba my own Principal had to assist a midwife in delivering a local woman's child – a practice which has now largely been shunned by the medical community. However, when no medical services are available, babies still have to be delivered. Interestingly enough, it seems that many people are still unaware of the important role midwives played in the development of pioneer settlements. Without their services, many more babies would certainly not have seen this world.

Otterburne, in the southeastern corner of Manitoba, where this story really begins, in spite of being one of the first towns on the Prairies, was, and to a large extent still is, a small nondescript farming community where, in those days, everyone knew and greeted each other by their first name and where all races, French, Galicians, English, Germans, First Nations and Metis, among others, would co-exist, intermingle and come together with little apparent friction or fanfare – a place where barn dances were regular Saturday night occurrences in some farmer's loft. As well, it was also a place where cattle, horses and oxen could be seen sharing the roads with the occasional self-propelled automobile which, strangely enough, at the time, stood out as sore thumbs as most of them had been turned into buggies and were now humbly being pulled by horses or other beasts of burden. Few people, it seems, could afford to pay even the few cents a gallon it took to keep them going – a problem, furthermore, compounded by the lack of suitable roads. So, rather than scrap them, as well as to protest the appalling conditions existing then, they had been stripped and turned into what were sarcastically referred to as Bennet buggies so-named after the Prime Minister who had borne the brunt of the blame for the misfortunes of the times.

At one end of town, in typical rural Western style fashion, stood a blacksmith shop and a stable where horses, or oxen, for a small fee, could be shod, watered and fed while the weary travelers went about their business in town. A general store which carried and sold everything one could possibly need and more – or afford – stood conspicuously and a bit imposingly in the centre of town and often served as the only available meeting place. Next to it, a small hotel with a bar awaited the thirsty traveler – provided he could afford the mere pittance for a mug of ale – or the occasional moonshine so popular then.

But it was really the church which caught the attention of all those who arrived in town. In fact, whenever towns were started in the wilderness, church buildings were among the first structures to be erected and blessed by the local priest and stood out conspicuously as a sort of focal point around which the rest of the town would eventually grow. And located, as it generally was in the middle of town – in this case directly across the general store which it more than rivaled in size – with its tall, awe-inspiring spire and immense cast-iron bell, it was an impressive site to behold. It could, not only, be seen for miles and miles around but also heard as well and often guided lost and weary travelers to their destination in such a vast, uncharted land. I remember, years later, from our own farm in LaBroquerie further east, at a distance of over six miles from the Church, we could easily spot the spire especially when the sun shone on it at just the right angle. In addition, which was probably more important, it also often served as a beacon of hope for many a parishioner where hope was the only commodity everyone could purchase at no cost. It was even hinted that one of the reasons the churches were so well attended was that they allowed people to forget the incessant drudgery and misery of their daily lives – even if for only brief periods of respite. And yet, this land was still far superior to the land my parents were fated to move to.

My mother, a rather saintly and extremely devout woman, god

rest her soul, had been raised in the adjacent Canadian province of Saskatchewan – a province which had come on its own in 1905 when it had separated from yet another adjacent province, Alberta. Together, they had made part of what was then known as the Northwest Territories, a region which had originally been ceded to Canada by the Hudson's Bay Company which had been given sole rights to the land – then called Rupert's Land - in 1670 by Great Britain. Saskatchewan was, and still is, a province of huge grain farms and gently rolling plains which has always produced an abundance of cereal grains for its citizens and the world at large. Unfortunately, during the Great Depression years, the land had not only suffered the ravages of droughts and strong prairie winds leaving vast areas covered with dust – and the occasional thistle and tumbleweed – thus earning it the apt nickname of 'the dustbowl' but had also been witness to devastation and mayhem at the hands – or mouths – of the ever multiplying and advancing hordes of giant locusts which visited the area every few years. My own father had once described them as miniature aircrafts continuously and mercilessly making their way across entire battlefields and destroying everything in their paths.

In spite of this, however, the timeless delicate flower of budding romance, no matter how dire the situation, still found time to blossom here and there. Courtships, however, were never long drawn-out affairs as they generally are today. There was just not enough time for that. And so it had been with my parents. The two had met and, with little apparent pomp and fanfare, gotten married when Dad had returned from following the rails West, as it was called, like so many young unemployed men did at that time, in search of work to try to put an end to their impoverished lifestyles or simply to supplement their own meager living on the family farms. As soon as he had acquired enough money working on the docks in Vancouver, British Columbia and the vineyards of the Okanagan Valley on the lower mainland, he too had returned home with a few extra dollars in his pockets to his family farm. Shortly after getting married with the woman who would forever remain the love of his life, they had started quietly and dutifully to plan for their future together in a frontier land in which neither of them could predict the dire consequences. Had they made the wrong decision? I'm sure that probably never crossed their minds as they saw it as their destiny at the time. Time, it would soon become apparent, however, was not to be kind to them as with the thousands who had made the same journey. But then, such were the risks.

Shortly after my older brother was born, Mom and Dad had decided to leave Otterburne as the land there, although better suited for agriculture, had been all occupied, and proceed to buy, with the money they had now acquired, some land further east. It was located on the outskirts of a little isolated hamlet known as LaBroquerie deep in the very heart of what was then truly a rugged and untamed wilderness. The soil where my parents were forced to settle, for the most part, was of inferior quality, being highly acidic, sandy, somewhat porous and easily eroded – the more so as trees were being cleared away for planting crops. This soon proved disastrous, especially in times of floods, droughts, heavy winds and the arrival of ever-hungry armies of grasshoppers, commonly referred as locusts. However, at the time, I was later told, that was the only land my parents could afford. It would have to do. And this was where they reluctantly chose to begin their lives and raise a rather large family. Unfortunately, the stage was now set for the reign of poverty and misery which would soon indiscriminately sweep our entire family along with many other families in their paths.

Times, needless to add, were extremely difficult from the very beginning. Having no house yet to move into, my parents had been forced, for the first summer and late into the fall, to live, first in a small canvas tent in the open field under a canopy of twinkling stars and threatening clouds, then in a makeshift shack made of old discarded lumber while attempting to survive meagerly on a diet supplemented by nuts, berries, tubers and the odd stray deer or hare my dad could dispatch combined with a few vegetables my mom had hastily planted on their arrival until a house could be erected and a proper garden started. And being in the wilderness, Dad recalled the times he actually had to sleep with his rifle close by him as wolves, coyotes, bears and even the occasional cougars were particularly bold and aggressive then - it was, after all, their territory and they were, understandably so, not too keen on sharing it - and would not hesitate to raid the family's miserly possessions, even the family itself, if given an opportunity. Many times, Dad, upon hearing excessive howling and scratching close by, and no doubt prodded by Mom, had been forced to get up during the middle of the night and fire a few volleys at these menacing marauders who often came to within a few feet of their tent, fearing for his very life and that of his family. What actually possessed him to remain there is a question which only he could answer – if he actually had an answer at all.

Eventually however, with the grateful help of neighbors, themselves also equally – and some even more so – destitute, and other family members who had come to lend a helping hand, a rudimentary structure – some would even have called it a cabin – had been set up. It wasn't much, but it would symbolize a new beginning. At least, for now, there was protection against the wild animals lurking in the vicinity, as well as the numerous sudden thunderbolts, rainstorms and ravaging winds which erupted every so often and just as suddenly in that region. It took another year to build a stable large enough to properly house the little group of animals they had painstakingly managed to acquire. So, for the first winter, these animals had to endure the bitter winter housed only under a hastily built half-covered lean-to which was barely able to keep the winds at bay, let alone the cold. Needless to say, a few did not survive through the winter.

Five years after my brother's birth, my eldest sister was born in the largely Mennonite town of Steinbach which boasted the only hospital for miles around. As if she had been a good omen, it was at this time that life began to take a turn for the better and improve somewhat as the family was slowly settling in on the new farmstead. They had now acquired several more heads of cattle, a few pigs, chickens, a couple of horses, a sheep for wool, even a goat and, of course, now they had a stable to house them in. Life, however, was still very trying for the growing family. Just the simple task of going to the store for the bare necessities and the six-dollar monthly government family allowances for each child – the government's feeble attempt to encourage larger families - meant a twelve-mile hike, either walking or on horseback on the makeshift trails in the bush. In later years, I remember my mother telling me that if the government family allowance check had not arrived, she would immediately have no choice but to turn back and head home – minus, of course, any groceries. And ours, she often made it a point to remind me, was not the only family that depended on that allowance. I sometimes wonder if, during these times, my mother would not dream of the Saskatchewan home she had left behind. But then, I guess young love works in mysterious ways.

When my brother turned six years old, he began school. The school, aptly called St. Roch – a seemingly fitting name given the presence of the many rocks in the vicinity - was simply a small but sturdy box-like one-room building with three rows of double-seats for the students, a make-shift wooden desk for the teacher, a few cupboards and a barrel-shaped furnace in the back for heat during those frigidly cold winter months. Fortunately, the school was built with a row of windows facing south-east allowing the warm rays of the sun to penetrate and provide some much needed additional heat. But, was it ever hot in the late spring and summer! But then, freezing and sweating were all deemed part of the learning experience in those days – although what these taught us was never really clear.

Also, it was not uncommon in the winter mornings before classes started to see students frantically scurrying around the building in futile efforts to keep from freezing. I know because I did it many times and, while I succeeded in sweating in the process, my hands and feet always seemed to remain cold – bitterly so. But then, I guess, rubber boots and thin mittens don't retain much heat in minus thirty and forty degree temperatures. Eventually, someone would arrive, and like long-awaited saviors in the numbing cold, start the furnace. About an hour or so later, you could just begin to feel the heat, and, one at a time, your fingers and toes. However, our first classes were usually taken with our jackets – and mitts – on until it became warm enough to take them off. That was the stuff which made real men and women we were often told. And, of course, at the time, we all believed that. Who knows, maybe there was some truth to it.

Transportation to and from school, also, presented a problem. Living over three miles from school, it was often impossible to simply walk there, especially in an area frequented by predators always on the lookout for an easy meal – and our lunch buckets would do just fine. At first, Dad had to escort my brother on horseback, then return to work on the farm until he had to go back and pick him up. If my brother, and later, the rest of us ever became sick at school it was too bad as there were no phones in these days. Later, Dad built a cart on two wheels which could easily be pulled by one horse and thus traveling became easier and more comfortable. However, being fitted on two wheels meant that it had to be harnessed properly to the horse to balance it before anyone could get in it — for obvious reasons. For the winter months, a sleigh with runners had been rigged up. Oftentimes, however, the deep snows made the trails impassible. Later, when my sister began school, she and my brother would travel together to school on their own as my brother was now old enough to lead the horse. That, of course, was not without its hair-raising moments as many a time the horse and sleigh would return home — minus its occupants. My sister later told me that while my brother was old enough to lead the horse, his lack of maturity had failed to keep up. He loved to goad the horse and it was exactly these shenanigans which often separated horse and occupants. Fortunately, my brother and sister had always managed to make it back home safely. Later on, I would join my sister on these excursions. By then, my brother had left school to seek work.

Chapter 3 – The Family Expands

As my sister before me, I was also born in the adjacent town of Steinbach, Manitoba. A few days before my birth, my dad had driven my mom to the closest hospital in the vicinity. It had been a particularly hot and humid day when my parents undertook this trip. At a distance of only about fifteen miles, it would seem like a minor drive today – certainly less than twenty minutes. But things were different then, especially since the family didn't own a suitable car to make the journey. Shortly after moving to our homestead, my dad had purchased an old jalopy which had lasted only a few years before being consigned to a corner of the yard where it could 'rust' in peace. Besides, it had rarely been taken out on the road as it was always broken down – and then only during the summer when the roads were dry. Later he would use the chassis to make a wagon to haul lumber. So the entire trip to the hospital had to be undertaken in a horse-drawn cart.

Here is how my Dad later revealed to me the events surrounding my birth. Early in the morning, he had hitched up his favorite horse, Blacky, to the cart and, picking Mom up, proceeded toward Steinbach. It proved to be an eventful trip on the slippery mud-covered trails in the bush which passed off as roads at the time. As it had been a particularly wet spring, the cart would continually slide sideways often forcing Blacky to veer to the right or to the left as necessary to compensate while, at the same time, having difficulty negotiating the potholes left by the falling rain. And to make matters worse, that year, there was an-earlier-than-usual infestation of mean little black flies which could administer serious pain and discomfort to any animal – or human – unable to protect itself. And all old Blacky had to fend off those ever-present voracious little blood demons was her tail which, as was often the practice then, was always kept short. There were times, it seemed, when all she wanted to do was turn back home to the relative safety of the stable. At least there, the full fury of these blood sucking little vampires was largely contained outside. No wonder, the year of '48 was remembered by the locals as a particularly momentous year for the black fly.

With a self-made whip in one hand and the reins held firmly in the other hand, Dad was also not immune to the stings of these miniature vultures. By the time he had arrived at the hospital, he had probably spilled as much blood as his mare. Mom, for her part, had been bundled up and well protected from the swarms of black flies but she had another problem to contend with – the heat. And it was hot! They say that trouble comes in threes. Well, first it was the rain, then the black flies and mosquitoes which followed and then an unusually early heat wave had very unexpectedly hit the region and was settling down with a near intolerable oppression. Old-timers talked of early temperatures in the high 80's and low 90's throughout most of the summer. No wonder I became so irritable later in life.

Back home, my older brother who was then almost nine years old and my sister who was four years old had stayed behind in the care of an elderly neighbor – the very woman, I was told, that I later had the nasty habit of punching in the stomach. Why, I don't know! Some thanks for a woman who had devoted herself to our care as we sometimes proved to be too much of a handful for our mother. Anyway, with a distance of fifteen miles to cover to get to the hospital, it was decided that it would be impractical to bring my older siblings along. What, if anything happened along the way? Besides, the extra weight, as well as the resulting whining and crying, could make it more difficult on my parents - and old Blacky who was getting on in years and slated to be set free soon to roam the pastures at will, until she was eventually sold to some abattoir for meat and replaced by technology. For some time now, Dad had been entertaining the idea of buying another used car. The problem, however, was that with the condition of the roads, a car, even one he could depend on, would still prove even less valuable than a good mare. And in the winter, with the amount of snow accumulating, it would be virtually useless. Anyway, Dad decided that he needed a car, presumably to make him feel that he was slowly moving up the ladder of success – albeit one slippery rung at a time. Just in case, though – and luckily for us, as we would later make great use of them, especially in the winter - he had kept a couple of younger horses to replace Blacky.

As soon as the muddy dirt road had been left behind and Blacky could feel sand and gravel under her hooves, she seemed to take on a new allure – a sort of second wind. Her gait now seemed to be firmer and quicker. Walking became more bearable. She even started trotting and, as this seemed to be effective in warding off the flies, she kept this gait for quite some time until finally, utterly exhausted, she had to revert to walking this time with both her head and tail working full-time to swish away those pesky black flies. Finally, the wind picked up a bit and these pint-sized vultures just seemed to vanish. Unfortunately, the darkening ominous clouds overhead were announcing an incoming storm – a definite reason for concern. It was now imperative to get to the hospital as soon as possible. Blacky seemed to sense the urgency and picked up her pace again, prodded no doubt by the sound of a cracking whip telegraphing the excruciating pain it could inflict if necessary.

Three and a half hours after leaving home, the buggy pulled up in front of the hospital amidst cars and a few other buggies, many of which, Dad said, belonged to a Hutterite community which lived nearby. Dad proceeded to tie up old Blacky to a post and help Mom from the cart to the hospital where they were greeted at the front desk by white-gowned hospital staff. After the necessary preliminaries, Mom was whisked away to her room where she would await my birth. In the meantime, Dad would have to make the return trip back home with Blacky – a trip certainly neither one of them was looking forward to.

About three days later, I was born and weighed in at a little over seven pounds. A day after that, Dad, who had heard the news from the local priest at church, appeared at the hospital. That day, however, he had arrived with his younger brother, my future godfather, as he had an important piece of business to conduct in Steinbach and, this time, he would not be returning home with old Blacky. He would finally be buying that automobile he had been dreaming about. It turned out to be a shiny blue 1946 Buick.

The return trip in the Buick made the journey seem a lot shorter but no less hazardous. These so-called cattle trails which appeared as soon as the gravel road from Steinbach ended proved a real challenge even testing Dad's own ability to manoeuver his new pride and joy. The problem of black flies had disappeared and since it had not rained for the last few days, the roads were relatively dry. But if anyone has ever tried to navigate dry, sandy mud-caked roads even with a car, especially one not equipped with proper shocks and springs, it soon becomes clear that it is not just a stroll in the park. It was so rough, Dad told me, that the car had to be geared down and allowed to move at the fast speed of about five to ten miles an hour for my benefit. However, for Dad, the chance of riding in a vehicle instead of in a horse-drawn carriage far outweighed the disadvantages of the slow headway made. Within about less than an hour of leaving the hospital, all three of us had finally arrived back home safely to be greeted by the other family members.

Over the years, there were to be four other members added to the family – a set of rambunctious, fidgety and high-spirited twins who had the unambiguous distinction of always getting into mischief and blaming the other – and the tricks they later played on their unsuspecting teachers and classmates have become legendary - a somewhat quick-tempered and equally highly-spirited, at times, volatile, younger brother who held the dubious distinction of being crowned with a unique tuft of white hair surrounded by thick auburn brown hair and another younger sister who, beside becoming the pride and joy of the entire family, often became the butt of pranks administered by her older male siblings.

Surprisingly for the kind of lifestyle we were exposed to, everyone was in reasonably good health and remained so throughout most of their lives. And, of course, as the family was growing up, one can well imagine that there was never a dull moment around with so many people crowded under the same roof – one could even say, a bit like the Walton's. As well, the little farmhouse that Dad had built when he had first purchased the farm soon became wholly inadequate for a growing family. It wasn't long, though, that again with the help of neighbors, the little house was gradually expanded. It soon boasted a concrete basement - where the furnace was installed - to store, among other things, canned goods, potatoes and anything else one could think of, a main floor and an attic where the bedrooms were located. There were three large bedrooms, one to be shared by the boys, one for the girls – a bit smaller – and one for Mom and Dad. In later years, another bedroom would be added on the main floor. It was in this modest and humble little castle in the wilderness that the family was raised until, eventually, one by one, everyone had moved out – but in body only, never in spirit. In spite of the many hardships we had had to contend with, we had done it together and in our hearts and minds at least, as long as this little cabin endured, it would always be home for us regardless of who lived in it.

As a result, it was a closely knit family that eventually surfaced to the outside world – the product of frugal living, hard times, and good, sometimes harsh, country discipline. Everyone had to learn to work together or suffer the consequences immediately – a long 3-inch wide leather strap hanging in a very conspicuous corner in the house was testimony to that. I guess, it was either now or later in life.

To keep this little growing family fed, every spring, Mom, would try to make sure that every summer the garden was filled with vegetables of every kind – peas, carrots, turnips, tomatoes, potatoes, cucumbers, radishes and a whole host of others. In addition, in later years, there was another garden plot added just for potatoes, being the one staple which everyone enjoyed year-round. And what wasn't consumed or ravaged by storms, droughts or insects – or wild animals – during the summer months, was canned and stored for the winter months thus ensuring, most of the time, at least a meager supply of foodstuff to last a large part of the winter. Also, every fall, Dad would butcher a steer or an older cow to provide us with meat. Unfortunately, with so many mouths to feed, that also would not go very far and we could simply not butcher every cattle on the farm. However, it did help to alleviate our reliance on store-bought groceries for which we had very little cash to purchase anyway. I also recall that we even had our own churn which we shared with neighbors to make our own butter. Back then, people quickly learned to be largely self-reliant or suffer the harsh consequences. Constant toil, resourcefulness and vigilance were the only guarantees against outright starvation, a fact driven home too readily then.

To the south of our little homestead at a distance of about one mile, lived an elderly farmer with his wife and grown-up son. Oftentimes, they would come and visit us later in the evenings when the chores had been done and stay to chat or play cards until the wee hours of the morning. This would provide one of the few forms of entertainment available on cold winter nights and affordable to us then. But one day, these visits simply stopped. The old guy had suddenly and without apparent warning just passed away – probably of old age. A period of sadness and loss spread throughout the family which was further exacerbated when shortly afterwards, his bereaved wife and her son sold the farm and moved away. When friends and neighbors are few and far in between such losses take on a greater significance.

Fortunately, they were soon replaced by a family with seven children. And while they were too young, at that time, to be ever considered as suitable playmates, I did spend many a night babysitting them thus earning for myself the huge sum of one dollar each night – not bad for about six hours work! Our closest neighbors, however, a family of German Mennonite immigrants – twelve members altogether – were about half a mile away. And as several of them were of our own age, it wasn't long before our two families would intermingle and could often be seen hiking that half-mile in either direction. Every summer, it was not uncommon to organize baseball games where one family would pit its skills against the other. As well, our two families together had the dubious distinction of making up over one-quarter of our school population.

We also had another neighbor, an elderly bachelor, who owned several horses, all of which, I remember, always appeared malnourished and grotesque-looking. But that never stopped us from gawking at them through the wire fence, and like scenes from movies, watching them interact with each other, sometimes kicking and sometimes biting each other with their two-inch long incisors – a truly scary sight. Our first experience with horror movies!

I recall a particular incident when, along with my twin brothers, I had been toying with the idea of approaching one of the horses. At last, I felt confident and brave or brash enough to approach one seemingly particularly friendly, or so I thought, cayuse. Since it was standing close to a mound of earth, leaves and packed manure, I decided it would be a relatively easy feat to jump on its back Roy Roger-style. No sooner had I landed on its rump than it bucked and reared its hind legs sending me catapulting up in a somersault causing me to land on my head on the half-frozen ground. After a few seconds, feeling a bit humbled by the experience, I casually walked away to nurse my sores in private. It had been extremely fortunate that I hadn't broken or twisted my neck. Needless to say, I then gave these equines a whole new respect and, of course, never attempted that daredevil stunt again.

Living, as we were, back then was a serious endeavor which often pitted life against death. Death, in fact, was everywhere around. All you needed to do was take long walks and you would come across carcasses of freshly killed or long dead and decaying animals. I have found many a skull and leg bones that way – it was a veritable archaeologist's cache. It was a fact of daily life and we were all too familiar with it. However, a kind of carefree abandon and happiness permeated our daily lives as well. Death was around us but you learned to tolerate it and get along with your life as best you could. It would be easy to say that such conditions were certainly not conducive to a healthy lifestyle. But, back then, that was all we knew or perhaps cared to know. Happiness came not from wealth and material acquisition but in the knowledge that you had a few like-minded friends and neighbors who understood you and with whom you could share your pain and sorrows as well as partake in the good times. Death was only a by-product of this way of life.

Nowadays, memories of these by-gone days have become mostly blurred but every now and then a few snippets of that past manage to penetrate through the sands of time and make their way into our subconscious. It is then that new stirrings become awakened within us forcing us to view these times from different perspectives. The passage of time has a peculiar way of discarding its negative aura and leaving us eager to explore that past. In other words, minds seem to work in mysterious ways – to borrow a well worn-out cliché – by being highly selective and hanging on only to what is truly memorable while discarding everything else. This helps explain why, long after the farm had been sold off and everyone had moved out, year after year, we would go back, in spite of the hardships and sorrows of the past – even when all the buildings had finally been razed to the ground. Was it just curiosity or nostalgia?

Chapter 4 – The old oak tree

I saw a live-oak growing,
All alone stood it and the moss hung down from the
branches,
Without any companion it grew there uttering joyous leaves
of dark green,
And its look, rude, unbending, lusty, made me think of
Myself,
But I wonder'd how it could utter joyous leaves standing
Alone there without its friend near, for I knew I could not.
Walt Whitman

One of my very first and most vivid memories as a child growing
up on the farm was also one of my most memorable. In the middle of the
field, about a quarter-mile from the family house, stood a colossal oak tree
in all of its majesty and magnetic beauty which had somehow inexplicably
managed to withstand the test of time. While everything around it had
gradually disappeared or been removed, it had, either through a slight
of the Almighty hand or good fortune, or both, somehow been allowed
to remain there relatively unscathed appearing ever defiant, ever stoic in
the very face of countless imminent dangers, from the swinging of the ax,
to insects, to lightning, even to the frequent tornadoes which visited the
area every year. In fact, with the passage of time, the tree had eventually
become a sign of guarded pride for the entire family symbolizing our
own unflagging determination to live and thrive on this half-vacant
piece of semi-barren land eschewing all types of hardships and hazards
which crossed our paths. It was truly a stroke of luck, a miracle perhaps,
certainly it was a mystery that a tree of its size, girth and stature had even
managed to thrive under these primitive conditions. But, it had. And as
long as this tree endured, we often claimed, so would we. And, we spent
countless hours under its shadow and protection contemplating our luck
that this image of royalty had actually seen fit to grow in our own midst.
Such trees, in the kinds of soil where we lived were simply unheard of.
Nowhere else could his equal be found. What a miraculous stroke of
luck we had thought!

I still vaguely recall the very first time I became conscious that such a tree was actually growing on the farm. I couldn't have been more than four years old at the time. My mother had taken me with her on an errand to deliver lunch to my dad who was, at the time, working in the field nearby with my older brother and sister. The twins, as they were generally collectively referred to, being too young to follow – as well as more than a handful to handle – had stayed at home under the care of a relative who would often live with us and help out with the chores.

We had just delivered lunch to Dad and my older brother and sister and were heading back home, me, seated in my rickety little discolored wagon playing with my home-made toys and Mom pulling it. I must have been playing for only about fifteen minutes – or so it seemed – when suddenly, I raised my head and there, right in front of me, stood that gigantic oak tree. Several times before, I had certainly passed by it – at least, I'm sure I had – and not once do I recollect ever noticing it. But this time, as if it had suddenly and inexplicably appeared out of the blues for my benefit, there it was, standing tall and erect, though a bit ravaged by time, with its outstretched tentacles like arms with crooked fingers waving seductively in the wind as if coyly inviting me to play with it. And the first thing I knew, my mother had propped me on one of the lower branches some of which, probably due to age or deformation, practically dragged to the ground.

I must have spent the better part of an hour scurrying up and down the lower tentacles under the watchful eye of my mother and exploring their every interesting knot and groove like an eager little monkey, even dragging some of my toys with me. Finally, to my dismay, it was time to leave. But every few yards or so as we headed home, I would look back with excitement and wonderment in the direction of that Lord of the Field, all the while beseeching my mom to take me back – but to no avail.

Ever since then, that tree became my own private little playground until eventually, I decided, willingly or not, that it was time to share my 'tree house' and proudly introduced it to my younger siblings letting them know, however, that I was still king of that castle – at least for a while. Unfortunately, a pair of fiery siblings hot on my heals working in tandem didn't relish taking a back seat for very long, as it were, and I eventually had to relinquish sole custody of my domain.

Even as recently as my late teens, I could often be spotted hanging around that tree until one day a vicious tornado probably guided by some unseen demonic hand bore down on it and unashamedly and very deliberately, it seemed, tore off its trembling tentacles and upper torso, partly uprooting it in the process and carelessly, even maliciously, abandoning its mangled body – all in a matter of seconds. Only parts of its decapitated and disheveled trunk remained attached to the ground when that tornado had completed its deed and left the area. I guess the end of the line for that tree had finally arrived. This was, without doubt, not only a bad omen for the family, a sign that our days on the farm too, perhaps, were numbered but also one of the saddest days of our lives, albeit only one of many more to come.

Ever since that incident, it has been impossible to walk where that tree had once stood so imperiously and, later, to revisit the farm without secretly shedding a tear or two for this old and dear friend who had entertained us for well over a decade guarding us vigilantly and tirelessly as we grew up. I had even secretly erected a small makeshift cross in its honor. When that tree was destroyed, it had been as if a family member had suddenly been taken away from us. And the sad thing was that nothing, not even weeds, ever grew on the spot where it had once stood so proudly. It was as if Mother Nature had had a change of heart and did not wish to provide nutrients ever again for new growth. However, I often wondered, if that tree could talk, what magnificent stories it could tell us about the family that grew under its wings.

In fact, that tree probably even saved my life one day. Ever since I was seven or eight years old, I would accompany Dad, and later, my younger siblings, to get the milking cows who were grazing somewhere deep in some small clearing in the forest and bring them back to the barn for milking. It was a task that would usually see me get up promptly at 5:30 every morning, seven days a week, and head out, in almost total darkness, toward the open fields bordering the forest still bathed only dimly in the receding light of the moon. In the distant horizon, you could just make out the first yawning rays of a waking sun. And every morning, like clockwork, you could actually feel and hear the deafening silence of the forest, like a scene from a horror movie, which was gradually and slowly being supplanted by the forlorn, distant plaintiff cry of the American Bittern proudly announcing the arrival of yet another new day. At the edge of this forest was where, hopefully, the cows had gravitated overnight and would be resting and ruminating peacefully after a long night of grazing, their location betrayed only by the occasional high-pitched sound of a metallic bell which one of them had appended around her neck. That bell, of course, had a dual purpose. It also served to warn predators that these cattle belonged to a farmer and should not be trifled with – at least that was our hope as we could ill-afford to lose any of them. Luckily, over the years, we lost very few cattle to predators. So it must be assumed that the bell was doing its job. Anyway, in my case, locating the cattle was only part of the problem at the time.

There was, to my frequent peril and anguish, one particular bovine – dubbed the mad cow – with a unique disposition, to put it mildly. Just as most families have an errant member, a black sheep, if you will, so does a group of cattle, at least this group did. This one had a tendency to charge and head-butt anything that moved, be it another cow, a dog or a human, especially a small and non-threatening one, even a tree, it made no difference.

One early morning, when I was returning to the barn with my Dad and our partly-crippled and partially blind canine companion, I was walking aimlessly, partly in a daze, half-asleep and had the misfortune of straying too far away from them, directly into the path of that lunatic cud-chewing machine. At first, she didn't appear to have noticed me and kept on, mischievously, jousting and squaring off with the other cows, until she spotted me. She must have thought what arrogance for this little sawed-off runt to approach the Queen in such a nonchalant manner. With one good snort and a few shakes of her massive hulking head, which announced that she knew I was there, she proceeded unhesitatingly head-long in my direction fully intent on doing me harm. Dad and our faithful canine companion, being on the other side of the little herd, had not seen what was about to transpire until I yelled out in desperation. But it was too late. All I could see were those enormously menacing shining round eyes and huge towering head single-mindedly bearing down on me.

Suddenly, I heard Dad cry out, "The tree! The tree! Head straight for the tree!" Reacting immediately, I turned around and, as fast as my spindly legs could carry me, I headed for the safety of the big old oak tree with that enormous steam engine closing in fast on me. The dog soon joined in by letting out a few of his blood-curdling barks. Unfortunately, even that wasn't enough to deter the steamroller intent on crushing the very life out of me. It seemed that this cow had realized long that this dog's bark was indeed worst than its bite. Finally, I managed to reach the tree and quickly ducked on the other side. Unable, or unwilling, to stop herself in time, the deranged cow ploughed directly into the tree frothing, or so it appeared, at the mouth while, like the scared little squirrel I was, I hightailed it up the other side of the tree as fast as I possibly could. Robbed of her potential victim, the cow just kept snorting and digging her hooves at the bottom of the tree as if scolding it for robbing her of her rightful prize. After taking a few futile jabs at the tree, she turned around and re-joined the herd as if nothing had happened.

It was then, I think, that Dad first came to the realization that this cow was just too dangerous to be allowed to run loose – a case of mad cow disease, perhaps? It took Dad a few years, however, to get rid of it as he needed all the milking cows he could get. In the meantime, the onus was on us to steer clear of that cow. Eventually, she was sold off and became hamburger on somebody's dinner table not before however, other similar incidents had occurred, not only to me but to my siblings as well. However, I shall never forget this incident, one which, perhaps strangely, made me appreciate the tree even more. After that, every time I noticed it standing by itself, forlorn and seemingly lonely, I would remember what happened and rush toward it to embrace it with all the might I possessed. In fact, I believe, at that point, it was then that I started, unbeknownst to my family, to see it as more than a mere tree. In my young, and perhaps naïve mind, I regarded it as a savior and gradually developed a special relationship with it. That was why I, among all my siblings, was particularly devastated when several years later it was ruthlessly destroyed.

Over the years, feeling sorry for its lonely existence, I would often uproot small shrubs and, along with some brightly colored flowers, re-plant them at the foot of the tree. Most, unfortunately, did not thrive but a few flowers did manage to survive – fooling Mother Nature – but were quickly gobbled up by rabbits and other rodents who frequented the area. I guess what wasn't meant to be just wasn't meant to be. It was a tree which, seemingly, had always been destined to a lonely and solitary existence – very much like our family was – until its unfortunate demise years later.

Chapter 5 – Tiger – The little dog with a big heart

For a man, his Creator is his God,
For a dog, his Master is his God.
Author Unknown

The very first time I laid eyes on her I was nine years old and, along with the rest of the family, fell in love with her instantly. There she was with those big floppy ears and sad but bright piercing yellow eyes, her proud regal chest thrust forward and her head held up high denoting a sort of aristocratic bearing. Her yellowish-brown hair, covered with just a few wisps of white stripes, seemed to glisten constantly in the sunlight and her small but powerfully built, sinewy muscles definitely marked her off in a class of her own. She wasn't a huge dog by any means but would unhesitatingly take on any dog twice her size.

A few months ago, Tiger's predecessor, having now become a bit unfriendly to us kids, that is, to all of us except, oddly enough, my youngest sister who could usually approach him any time, had to be done away with. For the rest of us, he had become a bit of a nuisance as it was becoming more difficult even to enter our own home which, as the guard dog he was, he jealously guarded by baring his still formidable fangs and letting a guttural growl which had the ability to send us scurrying in a panic.. Of course, our teasing him had not helped matters any. Unfortunately, the law of the land required that he had to go. He was shot by one of our neighbors who, I remember, had taken on the task in order to test his new firearm. I still recall the incident. Not being a very good marksman, he had shot three times – at least once in the leg - before the poor animal finally succumbed to its wounds. In spite of being the way things were done then, I can still too vividly recollect that whole scene that day as it enfolded on the edge of our farm, within eyesight – and earshot - of the house. It certainly wasn't a pretty scene, even then. And, as was the custom with dead farm animals, it had been unceremoniously buried the very same day. A deep enough trough in the ground had been dug up to prevent predators from sniffing the cadaver, the dog dropped in, then covered and raked over carefully to try to disguise the location. Shortly afterwards, the family went on the lookout for a replacement. And when Tiger came along, it was love at first sight. Not only was she an impressive canine specimen easily captivating our young minds and hearts at the time, but, unlike her predecessor, she had taken an instant liking to the entire family as we had with her.

Over the next few weeks, we took turns taking her everywhere on the farm helping her to familiarize herself with it by allowing her to sniff every possible nook and cranny. She was, after all, slated to be a guard dog – a sentinel – above all else forever on the lookout for any wild predator which might be brave or foolhardy enough to stray too close to the family as well as to the farm animals. Hopefully, they would just have to look elsewhere for their food now that Tiger was on the prowl.

Venturing far from the house, even in broad daylight, was always risky for us kids, especially unaccompanied by a good dog. Tiger's predecessor had performed his role well but as a young pup he had made the unfortunate mistake of getting too close to a young filly, and had been kicked on the side of the head. He was never the same after that. Later, either as a result of getting older or suffering from some bone crippling disease, he began limping. We knew then that his days were numbered. Perhaps, it was also at this time that his demeanor had changed. Sadly, it took a bullet to put him out of his misery.

When Tiger arrived on the scene, it was imminent and just a matter of time before we would be out there frolicking around in the forest. The forest, in spite of its potential and very real dangers, was always attractive with its numerous sounds, smells and colors which captivated our senses and gave free rein to our thoughts. And all the while, as we pranced around, Tiger would sniff here and there ever on the lookout for anything interesting that moved – even the occasional buds which fell from the trees. Tiger, it seemed, soon had the situation pretty well under control as rarely did we see any wild animals lurking about when she was around. Even the ever-present wacky jackrabbits thought it wiser to observe from the safety of their own burrows. It was as if predators, as well as their prey, had realized that infuriating Tiger, in spite of its diminutive size, could have repercussions. And so it remained for several years until the winter day I decided to go hunting with her.

I was about eleven or twelve years old at the time. Having gone hunting occasionally with my Dad ever since I was about seven years old, it was not uncommon for me to use one of my father's rifles and do some practice shooting on my own or with my brothers at the edge of the forest. In fact, then, most boys were practically weaned on firearms in case of necessity. That day, however, as I had done a few times before, I decided that I would go hunting by myself inviting Tiger to tag along for company, I wasn't too worried about predators since it had been my experience that most wild animals seem to possess a sixth sense when someone is walking around with a loaded rifle and tend to keep their distance. It's as if somehow they know the deadly nature of firearms and give them all the respect they deserve. One can only wish that humans would also have enough common sense to do the same. Today, however, as I was about to find out, a strange thing was about to happen. Something would lure the predators out of hiding and put them directly in my path.

Early Saturday morning, after chores, I packed a small lunch and headed out with Tiger on my heels eagerly anticipating shooting a small whitetail or at least a pesky jackrabbit or two. But that was not to be. I must have been walking for several hours munching on a bologna sandwich and still hadn't seen even any trace of any game - animal or bird. I was starting to be a bit frustrated so I stopped to rest, finish my sandwich and just frolic around with Tiger who, for some strange reason, seemed to be particularly agitated as if she were sensing that something was not quite right.

Unfortunately, I didn't pick up on this until it was too late. After a few minutes, I decided to resume my hike rather than return home empty-handed. It wasn't long, however, before I detected a few fresh tracks in the snow and bent down to try to identify them. To my utter surprise and consternation, they did not appear to be deer or rabbit tracks as I had hoped. They looked more like wolf or cougar tracks. Luckily, I could see only two sets of tracks and, with Tiger, I was sure we could dispatch, or at least scare whatever had made them if need be as long as we kept at a safe distance. Anyway, I kept on going in the hopes that they too were on the trail of a whitetail or some hapless jackrabbit. Maybe, I thought, I would cash in on their sense of smell. But, boy was I in for a surprise, one which could very well have cost me my life, if not for Tiger. I now know that it had been foolish of me to pursue these tracks, but we seemed to be more daredevilish then. Today, I probably would have simply headed back home, then and there.

The tracks led down to a gully adjoining an area which had been dubbed 'coteau a Robert', a small grassy promontory on the edge of the woods where game such as whitetail would often congregate in small groups to feed on the thick grass growing there – accompanied, of course, by a few predators waiting for their chance to pounce on one of them. As I leaned over to get a better look at them, I realized to my horror, that they were definitely not deer or rabbit tracks. It was only then that I thought it was best to hightail it out of there as fast as I could. Unfortunately, it proved to be too late. I had been spotted – or rather I spotted them. At that very moment, I realized the sheer cunning and craftiness of these predators which had developed over thousands of years of chasing prey. I had been duped and lured into their lair but the object of their desire, so to speak, was not I, at least not entirely, or maybe not even wholly, but Tiger. Wolves, especially the black timber wolves, being highly territorial, will never tolerate an affront or infringement on what they consider their territory by another animal not of their immediate family kin-group, whether another wolf, a coyote or a domestic dog. It seems that these wolves had probably been biding their time and were now keen on eliminating the competition and anyone else that stood in their way.

Looking out in the distance, I could count five of them – there could have been more – certainly too many for Tiger, feisty as she was, to take on. Domestic dogs have been known to tackle predators twice their size when defending their master – that is what sets them apart from other animals, very much like a mother bear defending her cubs from a much larger boar. Wolves, for their part, I knew, often work in tandem, two will rush in then two others will replace them. They had, over millennia, evolved into highly efficient killing machines and the thought of them ganging up on Tiger and ripping her apart, at first made my blood curdle. Then, came an immediate rush of adrenaline. Tiger, for her part, as if not showing or sensing any fear, had bared her fangs and refused, perhaps foolishly, to cower even at the sight of all these predators who were slowly, in spite of my firearm, and deliberately approaching from downhill, albeit appearing a bit reticent or cautious as if somewhat unsure of the fighting prowess of their adversary – or maybe of my presence. Wolves, like any wild predator, will do their utmost not to incur any wounds as these could very well ensure a very cruel fate later on down the road. It was then that I realized that, were it not for Tiger, I might have been easily dispatched by the group had it wanted to – although I had never heard of wolves attacking humans before. But this was a special circumstance. I was practically at their front door as an uninvited guest. In spite of their reluctance to rush head on, I knew I was definitely not out of the woods yet.

Suddenly, it came to me and Tiger's bluff had given me just enough time to think about it. I had heard somewhere that once the leader of the pack – the alpha male – is dispatched, the rest will turn tail and scatter – at least for my sake and Tiger's, I had hoped they would. Slowly, I looked over all of them until I spied the big male crouching on all fours and presumably getting ready to make his headlong rush. Slowly as if suddenly remembering that I had my rifle, and with all the fanfare I could muster, I cocked it noisily and pointed it directly at him and made sure he could see and hear me. At that point, appearing a bit startled by the turn of events and a bit unsure of himself, he stared directly at me, making eye contact, immediately sending shivers up and down my spine. And somehow, I don't know how or why, as if just coming out of a transfixed daze, he seemed to realize what was about to transpire.

With what sounded like a pitiful, even playful, puppy-like whimper, he buried his head in the snow then got up, seemingly having forgotten about Tiger and turned tail soon to be followed by the rest of the pack and headed for the safety of the bushes with Tiger becoming bolder and growling even more defiantly as the pack receded. Shaking uncontrollably at this point, I called out to Tiger who now seemed intent on following them into the bushes then soothingly rubbed the back of her head gently praising her as I did so. Then, I reluctantly but wisely headed home and forgot about hunting for a while – but never about that incident.

Animals, I believe, especially those of the canine variety, possess an uncanny ability to remember experiences and use them to plot their future decisions – these wolves had certainly proven that. This power which we call instinct, however, seems to be only one facet of their individuality. The ability to think and plan, at least on some elementary level, seems to be another. One only has to observe them in their natural habitat to realize the unique power of their intellect. As time passed,

Tiger, coming from a long line of domesticated canines whose forebears reached far back in time to her wolf-like ancestors would do no less. She now appeared to be more on her guard than ever as if remembering this encounter and was often spotted patrolling her territory barking toward the direction the incident had taken place and giving one the unmistakable impression that any predator or prey unlucky or foolhardy enough to cross her sight or territory would be made short-shrift of. While it may still not have been safe to venture very far in the forest, it was perfectly safe anywhere else on the farm. Oddly enough, even the cattle seemed to sense that.

There was one time, however, when Tiger inadvertently put herself in a precarious and perhaps even life-threatening situation. And it wasn't with a large predator but with a rather small, smelly but highly territorial mother skunk. It happened only about a hundred yards from the house in the tall grasses growing there – a place generally frequented by mice, frogs, snakes and other small animals. Apparently Tiger had never encountered a mother skunk before and wasn't too sure how to handle it. After all, she must have thought to herself, it was only a small creature and what harm could it possibly inflict on her. That was something Tiger was soon to find out.

It was early one Sunday afternoon – I remember that because we were about to go berry-picking – and Tiger could detect some movement in the grasses as she was making her usual rounds. Curiosity got the best of her and she just had to take a closer look and investigate. Suddenly, without apparent warning, a warm choking mist shot out and hit her directly in the face. Well, that's all it took and, after a few gasps and coughs, the chase was on. The skunk would run a little then lift its tail and let out another volley. And each time, Tiger would derisively wipe her face on the ground. This went on for a while until finally, it seemed, as I couldn't really tell from where I was standing, the skunk had run out of mist.

That was when apparently Tiger decided to take the opportunity to pounce on her prey – a near fatal error on her part. Even a skunk that has dried up is still a very formidable foe as Tiger would soon find out. Just as she opened her jaws to grab the skunk by the nape of its neck, the skunk somehow succeeded in turning over or was knocked upside down. As it went down, it managed to sink its small but formidable teeth in

Tiger's exposed throat and held on firmly for dear life. In spite of shaking the skunk with all her might, Tiger could not succeed in dislodging it from its deadly embrace. This life and death struggle went on for quite a while until it seemed that Tiger was running out of steam and the fight was slowly leaving her body drained. For a while, it appeared that the skunk not only had the upper hand but might actually vanquish its foe. As I edged closer, I could only stand there frozen, transfixed on this life and death struggle that was now ensuing before my very eyes, unable or too afraid to help Tiger.

But it seemed that the skunk, too, was running out of steam – and perhaps Tiger was sensing that and just playing possum waiting for the right opportunity to make a move. Just as it appeared that Tiger was ready to give out, she tensed her small but mighty muscles, gave one last tremendous shake of her head and up in the air like a rag doll catapulted the stunned skunk. Immediately, without wasting any time, Tiger sank her teeth in its throat and that was it for that skunk. But for quite a while, Tiger just lay there panting and bleeding profusely from the neck and reeking from such a foul odor that no one dared approach her for quite some time. This, however, was another lesson that Tiger was never likely to forget. In the future, she was often observed giving wide berth to skunks content only to bark at them from a safe distance.

Chapter 6 – And the work goes on

We have sweat our share;
The harrow is caught full of sod-pieces,
The bright disks are misted yellow in the wet earth,
Hear tardy hesitant drips from the eaves!
Let the rain work now.
We are not done with toil;
Let rain work in these hours,
Wind in night's hours,
We with the sun together
Tomorrow
Raymond Knister

Providence, we believed, had, for reasons unknown to us, been unfair – certainly, growing up, we all felt that way. It had dealt us a harsh and cruel hand as if mischievously taunting us and ensuring that our lot be one of perpetual and seemingly never-ending slavish deference to a land which, in spite of our blood, sweat, and yes, even our occasional tears, was not prepared or willing to bear much fruit, as it were. Day after day, month after month and year after year, the same monotonous tedium would play itself out and we would dutifully – of course, what choice did we have – labor on and pour out our very hearts and souls in countless desperate and futile attempts to try to make it productive only, in the end, to resign ourselves, gather our sorrows, wipe our sweaty brows and gaze upon row after row of shriveled, bug-infested and half dead crops. And yet, somehow we would always find the energy, persistence and forbearance to pick ourselves up and continue. It was, after all, we would convince ourselves, our home and, I guess, we were determined even to defeat the gods themselves, if need be, and do battle against all odds. I suppose, just like lotteries nowadays, occasional successes – and there were a few, there had to be – spurred us on to try again in the hopes that eventually we would beat these odds and make all this perseverance finally pay off in the end. And, that's what it was like living on most pioneer farms then – certainly, it was, on our farm.

Of course, it has to be said that not all years were lost ones, though.

There were some which produced surprisingly abundant and healthy crops – albeit, only in a relative sense, and, in the process, raising our hopes and dreams that perhaps finally we would be able to see our way clear out of this seemingly never ending cycle of poverty. These were the years of plenty, to borrow a biblical phrase. Unfortunately, they were too few and far in between. But in the end though, due to our constant countless struggles, not only with the soil but with the elements as well and in spite of the sad fact that we had lost our own mother to this land, we could take some solace and comfort in the realization that the rest of us had come out of it, or so it seemed on the surface anyway, relatively unscathed and with a strengthened work ethic which would serve us well in the future when it came time for us to grapple with the outside world.

For most of us, the rigors of farm life began at a very tender age around the time we were about six or seven years old. I was barely six years old when I first started going out to the barn to help my dad and older brother and sister. Just a year or so later however, my brother would, around the age of sixteen, be encouraged to leave the farm and hire himself out on a more prosperous grain farm further west – quite a bit further, it turned out. This had always been the practice especially in communities where families tended to be disproportionally large in the hopes that they could provide an adequate labor force if and when needed to keep the farm going. Unfortunately, more often than not, it also tended to stretch the availability of the food supply on which the family relied to survive – hence, the reason for farming out, as it was then called, the older members of families.

So from that time on, unfortunately, my brother was rarely seen at home again except during these rare occasions when his new employer could do without his labor. This, of course, had the deleterious effect of alienating him, as well as a whole generation or more like him, from the rest of their families, and fostering a gradual loss of affection for the rest of their siblings. In other words, they felt they had been forsaken at a young age by those who should have nurtured them – their families. As a result, they would never really be able or have the necessary inclination to re-establish closer ties with the families they had been forced to leave behind. Some undoubtedly overcame that, but many didn't – at least not for a very long time. Of course without a doubt, my brother's life on the new farm was still extremely difficult, but at least he was assured three solid meals a day in return for his labor and a bit of money in his pockets. Such were the times. Besides, as harsh as this may sound, there was, now, one mouth less to feed. And when families are reduced to living from hand to mouth, as it were, this is no small achievement. It meant that there would now be a bit more for the others – a bitter reality in this austere land, but a sad fact of life nevertheless.

At first, my chores consisted mainly of cleaning the barn and feeding and watering the livestock. By the time I was eight, I started milking the cows – by hand. There were no milking machines in these days and, even if there were, we certainly couldn't afford them. So, every morning, seven days a week, after retrieving the cows from the fields, I would sit there quietly with my milk pail tucked firmly between my knees and milk, milk and milk. In the winter, of course, the cows would already be in the barn but that usually meant about an hour of back-breaking clean-up chores before finally sitting down and getting on with the task of milking. And in the evenings, after school, the same routine would play itself out all over again. That certainly didn't leave much time for leisure activities or other pursuits. Our only choice was to try to reserve the weekends for that. But then, somehow it always seemed, other chores popped up.

As our only source of heat for the house – as well as for cooking, baking and washing – was a large wood burning stove in the kitchen and a larger furnace in the basement to heat the entire house, extremely ineffectively, I might add, it was necessary that we gather as much firewood as possible to see us through the long cold and bitter winter months – hence the weekend chores. It was not uncommon for temperatures to plummet to minus 40 degrees Fahrenheit and linger for days, even sometimes weeks on end. As well, to make matters worse, snow would also accumulate against any building to a height reaching fifteen or twenty feet – good to slide on but nasty when these snow banks barricaded entrances and had to be cleared up – by hand shovel. Every winter, it seemed, without fail, anywhere we had to go usually meant countless hours of excruciatingly back-breaking shoveling before the chores could even be started.

Every fall, as soon as we had barely finished with the harvest which had occupied most of our time during the precious summer holidays, was the time when we would to turn our attention to getting the firewood to heat up our house. And a house poorly insulated with sawdust, which was the only cheap and readily available source of insulation at the time, certainly required a lot of heating to keep even moderately warm. In fact, waking up during the cold frigid winter mornings and seeing one's breath was not only common but also anticipated. I still remember trying to curl my lips and make little circles of condensation before struggling to put on my clothes.

Early Saturday mornings, after the chores had been completed and a hastily gulped down breakfast, we would hitch our inseparable duo, Nellie and Mud, to a specially rigged wagon and travel several miles deep into the forest where the best lumber trees could be found and proceed painstakingly to cut them down and strip them of their branches with an ax and a saw, then load them on the wagon. We would very often not return home with a load until it was time to do the evening chores.

This lasted for several weeks even throughout the first winter months. But now, instead of a wagon, we would switch to a sleigh for easier travel in the snow. And as soon as we had accumulated a suitable amount of wood or there was simply too much snow for the horses to travel through, then and only then would we stop hauling. Our greatest fear, of course, was always not to have enough wood to last throughout the long cold winters – and it happened, forcing us to lug heavy logs in the middle of winter in the deep snow. Meanwhile, in the evenings and even on Sundays, the only times we didn't haul any lumber we would take the saws out and cut the logs we had carted in and pile them neatly on the ground. In later years, we were fortunate enough to have rigged a pulley to a circular saw in front of the tractor and use the force of that pulley connected with a big leather strap to turn the saw. This made it a lot easier as well as a whole lot faster. But that constant ear-splitting buzz! Oh, how I remember it well! Even after leaving the farm several years later that penetrating sound had somehow attached itself indelibly to my memory and followed me like a lonely, eerie voice beckoning from a distant past. There are just some things from which it is extremely difficult to run away from.

Then came the countless hours spent splitting and piling the sawed lumber. And when this was done, we would then cart the wood off to the basement of our house where we would pile it again to make it available throughout the winter. During those frigid winter months when the snow would pile up everywhere and the temperatures would often be abnormally low, having this wood within easy reach was truly a godsend. Of course, if the house had ever caught on fire, it would certainly have gone up as easily as a tinder box. And, if it had happened in the middle of winter at night, where could we possibly have taken refuge? Certainly we couldn't just get in the car – even if we managed to start it – and drive away as oftentimes the roads were also covered with snow. That left only the horses. But imagine trying to harness fidgety horses to a frozen sleigh in the middle of a pitch black night illuminated by a burning house just a few yards from the barn as panic quickly set in – and it would! Even thinking of such a scenario still sends shivers up and down my spine. Certainly someone up there must have been looking out for us at the time.

Meanwhile back at the ranch, as they say, the cattle had to be watered and fed. And this, not surprisingly, was also a fairly long and drawn out process. As we had no running water then, all water had to be pumped by hand and carried pail by pail to a special drinking trough located inside the barn. And when one calculates that one thirsty cow can consume several gallons of water at a time, attempting to quench the thirst of a couple dozens of them several times a day was truly a daunting task. And as soon as this was accomplished, it was feeding time. For this, we had to go outside the barn, shovel any snow piled up on the hay, and, needless to say, there was usually a lot of it, then, with a pitchfork in hand, cart the hay inside to feed each cow – as well as making separate straw bedding for each one. And this had to be done every day, at least twice, all winter long until the snow disappeared and the cattle could finally be let out to graze on any newly-germinated grass which might be available.

As soon as spring rolled around the corner, other chores, as well, had to be performed. It was now time to start thinking about getting the fields ready for planting. Again, much to our disappointment, the greater part of our weekends would be used up for that purpose. Good-naturedly, albeit perhaps a bit grudgingly, we soon grew to accept that. We had, in fact, very little choice in the matter. While Dad did what he could during the week when we were at school, there was still a lot left for us kids to do on weekends.

As we were living on the edge of the forest region, there always seemed to be plenty of loose stumps around – even in the clearings. It seemed, to us kids anyway, that during the winter months they would somehow mysteriously work their way up to the surface and coyly stare at us, just in time for us to remove them in the spring. So for the better part of a week or two, we would be laboriously – again mumbling constantly as we did so – walking back and forth in the fields, often under a persistently searing hot sun while choking on the endless array of dust particles floating in the air – which seemed to constantly permeate the surrounding area around these dry desert-like soils – pulling out loose or partly loose protruding stumps, as well as the occasional rock, then discarding them in a wagon pulled by horses. I still very vividly recall bending down to pick up one stump only to spot a dozen more on my way up. There always seemed to be an endless supply of them. And only after this unpleasant task was finally accomplished – at least for another year – could the real work of preparing the land for planting be started. And, still now, I remember my Dad – actually I can still see him poring over the dust-filled field and wiping his brow, big straw hat in hand – always hoping that this was finally the year that would see the crops thrive as never before, only to be disappointed again and again in the end and resign himself to planning for the next year. It was truly a constantly never-ending, though, it must be admitted, one-sided tug-of-war with Mother Nature.

The first operation, once the fields had been cleared of debris, was plowing them to overturn that precious moist topsoil in the hopes that it would somehow magically release its life-giving nutrients to the crops that were soon to be planted. But sandy, acidic soil does not readily provide a lot of life-sustaining nutrients for young plants to thrive on. Unfortunately, however, this did not seem to deter the propagation of countless ubiquitous weeds and giant clovers which would very quickly take root and flourish crowding out the very crops we wanted to cultivate. And, as if this wasn't enough, the frequent droughts always occurring, it seemed, at the exact moment when the young sprouts could have used the extra moisture, administered further punishment to the land. Nonetheless, as they say, no matter how precarious and daunting the situation, life had to go on.

After countless hours of plowing, initially with two horses pulling the plow, then in later years with the use of a tractor, it came time to break up the overturned sod with a disk, then leveling it with a harrow. Reflecting back to these days, it now seems to me that a lot of labor and energy were being expended for the meager benefits which resulted. And being the eldest boy on the farm, for a number of years the bulk of this labor fell squarely on my shoulders while the rest of the family was busy with other less demanding farm, but no less necessary, chores.

However, one by one, as we got older, we all went through that same ordeal of working the land – our onlyguarantee against outright starvation in the wilderness. If the land didn't produce, what would become of us? That question was never very far from our minds. There was even talk, and, in fact, several attempts were made, to sell the farm. However, no one, to my recollection, ever stepped forward to buy it. This may explain why we never left the farm until we had each completed High School and were forced to seek our fortune elsewhere. Besides, in any case, where could such a large family have gone? Times were extremely difficult everywhere.

Seeding, which came next, was another labor intensive task which required great patience and, even, great accuracy. For several years, seeding was done by pacing back and forth from one end of the field to the other with a special apparatus attached to your body. As you turned a crank, the seeds would disperse in the field. The problem was that you had to notice where you had previously walked or some areas would get an over-abundance of seeds and others would be left bare. This method was employed for a few years until we had opened up too much land to make it feasible. So, as soon as we could afford it, my Dad had bought a used seed drill which, of course, he had to constantly repair but, at least, when it worked properly, could be pulled behind a tractor and dragged across the fields planting those precious seeds as it moved. New technology of some sorts was finally poking its head out and invading our little wilderness domain, at last!

Once the seeding was done, there was virtually nothing, except the usual farm chores, to do until harvest time but wait, pray and hope for good weather to come along. Either too much rain or too little could spell doom for our crops. And, unfortunately, even with the weather cooperating, the soil, by its very nature, was wholly inadequate to provide the necessary ingredients for the young growing plants. However, be that as it may, as they say, this period was actually one of the few periods during which we could actually have some free time – time we were always looking forward to and relished with gusto. It was a time when the entire family could finally look forward to picnic lunches, going to the beach or playing baseball games either together or with our neighbors for they too, were going through the same process at virtually the same time and facing the same rigors we were. Imagine doing that every year while growing up! In those days, that was what farming was all about. Holidays were unheard of.

Every year, as if we didn't have enough to preoccupy ourselves with, while we dreaded such cataclysms as flash floods, droughts, the menace of grasshoppers and black flies, one of our biggest horrors was without question, the arrival of the tornado season. Every tornado would always send us scurrying like frightened rats to the perceived and relative safety of the basement of our home. It was not unheard of to find out that after a tornado had passed through, several buildings had been completely demolished sometimes accompanied by the loss of not only farm animals but also of people who had been unfortunate enough to be caught in its path. While our house had been put on a concrete foundation, it had never been properly bolted down – as if that would have made any of us safer – so every gale or tornado threatened to shake if off its very foundations making it unsafe to stay in during these times.

I remember an evening when Dad had deemed it unsafe for us even to cower in a corner of the basement and had packed the whole family in our old car, thinking that it might be safer there. I also recall at that time, while peering out the window of the car during the waning hours of the night, one of our wagons being steadily pushed forward by the brute force of the fierce, howling winds and ramming into the fence nearby. It was then that I truly realized, maybe for the first time, the very real danger and precariousness of our situation. The thought, at that moment, that the car in which the entire family was cocooned could be next is another memory indelibly engraved in my mind ever since. That evening, however, death must have been close to knocking at our door since, our neighbor, fearing for our lives had braved the tornado and arrived with his big truck to take us to his place where we would spend the night. His house, being bigger and less exposed to the elements was deemed safer.

That night though, I recall, tornado or not, it had been a lot of fun for us kids as it was probably the only sleep-over we had ever had. The next morning was another story altogether. We had to get back home to do the morning chores. And trudging over half a mile through knee-deep thick gray sticky gumbo, which had accumulated overnight, before even beginning our chores quickly drove home our plight and the hardships we were forced to endure in this frontier environment. Luckily, it was a Sunday morning and the roads would make it impossible to attend Mass!

Chapter 7 – Predators, Predators and more Predators

Being raised in a wilderness setting makes one keenly aware early on in life of the potential threats posed by certain types of wildlife. And, of course, for families living in a region almost completely dominated by forest there was certainly no dearth of wildlife in the immediate vicinity. Every year, it was not uncommon to watch a variety of predators just strolling by – and sometimes stalking their unfortunate prey – within shouting distance of our house. Wolves, coyotes, bears, skunks, raccoons, badgers and the occasional cougar – this latter species having all but disappeared from the area recently – all paraded at one time or another. When that happened, Mom and Dad would usually make sure that everyone stayed close to the house. However, as years went by as we grew up, we gradually got a bit braver and ventured further out but ever vigilant of what we considered our competitors. Our worst moments were when we had to retrieve the cattle, oftentimes deep in the forest, for milking. Luckily, we always had our canine companion and, his constant barking usually deterred any would-be predator from approaching us – although you always knew they were lurking around. Some years it was the wolves that appeared in larger numbers, other years it was the coyotes, then the lynx, then the bobcat and so on – these latter species also have, of late, pretty much disappeared and gravitated to more northerly and safer regions. But during the years we lived on our farm, these predators had not yet learned to fear man and could pose a danger if we were not on our guard.

There was one year, however, which stood out particularly vividly in our collective memories more than any other as it affected most farmers in the vicinity and further around. That was the year when, for whatever reason, the black bears had been especially active and visible during the entire summer and throughout the fall. It may have been due to a lack of berries and rodents which they needed to feast on before winter set in. It may also have been due to the fact that some farmers had started setting up bee hives to produce honey as I recall many hives being overturned that year. Or it may also have been that there were many more live births than in previous years as these tend to follow cycles. Whatever the reason, farmers, that particular year – even the townspeople, who also were surrounded by forests which afforded good hiding places for predators – were overly anxious and worried about being attacked and mangled even in the perceived sanctuaries of their own homes. And, as some reports had indicated, some were, but these were rare occasions.

I remember a story circulating around then about a huge black boar which had broken into one of the houses while the adults were gone, carted away an unfortunate young child into the forest and was feasting on her remains when he was finally located and shot. Whether this story was true or not – most people at the time believed that it was, certainly my Dad did – families were especially on their guard that year and for years afterwards as such memories tend to fade slowly. Seldom would anyone even dare venture very far from home without a good firearm or a faithful canine companion. One neighbor, in fact, reported that one of his own cows had come close to being dragged down and mauled by one of these behemoths. The next morning, he swore he could see the claw marks running down her side. She had probably been grazing by a small bush, he claimed, when the bear pounced on her. Fortunately, she had not yet been de-horned and this may have provided a suitable means of defense against the predator who only managed to claw her. Whether it was a bear, a cougar or some other predator, he couldn't say at the time. Whatever happened, it was very obvious that agitation and fear were writ large on that farmer's face as demonstrated by his facial expressions as he recounted the incident.

There were also, that year, other reports which, I recall, fascinated and alarmed us at the time. Sometimes, it was difficult to distinguish fact from fiction as some people have a tendency to run away with these stories – no doubt our early cave ancestors had done the same thousands of years ago. Nevertheless, farmers all over the region kept a sharp lookout on their cattle and their own families. One particular story even related another incident where a huge bear had broken into a pig pen and carried away, in his arms, a 400-pound squealing sow in the forest. It seemed to us, however, even at our young age that these bears were certainly either getting bolder, bigger and stronger or the storytellers were getting better at their craft. Some stories, of course, were no doubt true but others, like this one, seemed a bit too fantastic even to our impressionable minds.

But that was how the seeds of alarm were being spread throughout the region. Eventually people became intent on doing something about it before the 'bear problem', as it was called, got out of hand. And when one farmer encountered a family of black bears – a sow and three cubs – casually sitting in his corn field in the middle of the day feeding on his prize crop, this seemed to be the proverbial straw that broke the camel's back. Bears, it seemed, had become more than a mere nuisance; they were now becoming a threat to the crops as well.

It was then that two brothers, who lived a few miles from our place, decided to go bear hunting and attempt, if nothing else, to scare these predators back deeper in the forest. That decision, unfortunately, had been hastily hatched after a few beers and perhaps the odd dare and had not been thoroughly planned or thought out. As a result, it almost proved disastrous for the brothers. Walking through the bush in pursuit of a mean, hungry bruin – or more than one – is not the wisest thing to do even if you are each carrying a firearm. But that was what they had decided to do. Their plan was simply to scour for tracks, scat or other telltale signs that a bear had been in the vicinity then climb a tree and patiently wait for it. They assumed wrongly that it would be that easy. Unfortunately, such events don't necessarily unfold as planned – even the best laid plans of mice and men can go astray, as the saying goes.

No sooner had they spotted their intended prey than, instead of climbing a tree which they should have done before being spotted and which could have afforded them some reasonable degree of safety, they apparently threw caution to the wind and decided to follow it at what they considered at the time to be a safe distance. That was their first mistake. For some reason, the bear had also detected their presence, turned around, and kept on steadily moving in their direction. Some bears, especially hungry and stressed-out ones, have been known to do just that – or maybe he was just minding his own business, we'll never know. And just at the fateful moment when they finally realized that the bear might actually be stalking them and was not about to turn back or veer onto another trail, suddenly, in their panic – perhaps the effects of the beer had just worn off – they could find no suitable trees around to climb. Instantly, one of the brothers, the younger one, thought that he had a good enough view to dispatch it and perhaps add a feather in his hat in the process – something to regale his pals with later over a cold bubbly. Anyway, getting down slowly and carefully on one knee, at least that is how he recounted it later to us, he boldly, albeit, I'm sure, a bit uneasily, took careful aim and fired a shot. As the bullet sped toward its intended target, he tried to follow its trajectory by listening to its echo as it whizzed through the forest breaking or snapping a few branches along the way.

Unfortunately, the bullet, as he soon realized, had just grazed the bear – probably, as he told us, due to the fact that it ricocheted on one of the overhanging branches. Anyway, that was his version and he stuck with it. Just then, the stunned bear gave out one of the most frightening and diabolically blood-curdling guttural growl they had ever heard and it did the unexpected. Instead of running off deeper into the woods, the stunned bear started charging in their direction. And, according to their later description of the event, boy, did it look mean! Turning several shades of white, the younger brother proceeded shakily to get ready to fire another shot. However, in his overzealous haste and excitement, he inadvertently jammed his firearm. No matter how much he tried, it would not fire as he could not successfully dislodge the empty shell. And there was that lumbering growling furry behemoth bearing down on him with its menacing jaws extended, its teeth bared, and certainly, with only one very predictable thing on its mind at that moment.

Fortunately, his older brother who was a few feet away had just finished loading his own rifle – another mistake which should have been taken care of before they set out in the bush and could have cost them dearly – and quickly fired a volley at the approaching bear hitting him squarely in the left shoulder. That caused the bear to stop dead in its tracks probably with a broken or very sore shoulder. This time, it turned around and headed deeper into the forest apparently favoring its right shoulder.

Of course, the proper thing for the brothers to have done at this time would have been to follow the wounded bear into the bush – an extremely dangerous thing to do – and finish it off. However, they were both too frightened and shaken up from the ordeal to pursue it any further. Their first thought was to get out of the vicinity as fast as possible. They had had enough and agreed that they would return later with reinforcements. In the meantime, having learned a new respect for Mother Nature, they quickly hightailed it out of there.

Fortunately, as luck would have, they never did see that particular bruin again. And that was alright with them. It may have crawled away and bled to death somewhere in the vast expanse of forest and been quickly gobbled up by the numerous vultures and other predators which lived in the area waiting for just such a feast. Or it may have met its end at the hands of another hungry bruin intent on satisfying its own blood lust. But this was one experience the brothers would not soon forget.

I still remember, as they reveled in the glory of recounting the story, even now that they were safe and far removed from the scene, how they were still shaking. The younger brother, I noticed, even had difficulty lighting up his own cigarette, so distraught was he from this incident. It could, of course, have ended very differently. Fortunately, they had learned a valuable lesson of the wilderness without having to pay a hefty price in return – except perhaps burnt pride – for their somewhat cavalier approach to such a potentially hazardous undertaking. That lesson was simply that the wilderness, regardless of its grandeur, can be very dangerous and unforgiving if you don't adequately prepare yourself for it and use common sense.

That year, due to the fact that so many hunters were out there trying to bag a few of these behemoths, there were many more bear encounters. In the meantime, people still had to get on with their lives but with ever greater caution and keeping an ever watchful eye toward the bushes. Some people were even encountering bears in their own garden patches which, even after harvest were still filled with discarded goodies such as rotting vegetables and berries – a veritable smorgasbord for hungry bears. This was one year in which people were hoping for an early snowfall which would send the bears into hibernation earlier. Unfortunately, before that happened, bears needed food or they would not last the winter. And many probably did not make it as the bear problem had decreased the following year. Anyway, in the meantime, they needed food. So, of course, farms, with their ever ready supply of fresh live poultry and young domestic livestock, continued to be a prime source of food for the bears' voracious appetites. But the farmers were equally adamant that their livestock remain theirs and many bears, that year, were either shot or went into hibernation, hungry.

One year, cougars seemed to be making their mark as they were being spotted more often. One day, my youngest brother was cutting hay about a mile from the family house when, from a short distance, he noticed something which looked like a branch fluttering in the wind. Upon approaching closer, he noticed, lying placidly on the grass, at the edge of a small bush, a lioness and two cubs. Luckily, he was on the tractor at the time so he just moved on leaving the family to enjoy its siesta. Cougars are generally not known to get so close to human habitation. However, they have been known to do so when food is scarce.

But, as usual, if it wasn't a bear or cougar problem, there was no scarcity of other predators to take their place raiding the more vulnerable farmsteads in search of food. Wolves and their smaller cousins, coyotes, I remember, were never shy at raiding our chicken coop during the middle of the night when everyone was sleeping. Over the years, we lost a number of chickens to them – even one of our prize roosters of which I was so proud of. It was a fact of life in the wilderness which had to be put up with. Even domestic dogs, which likewise, had to often forage for scraps of food, as well, would sometimes raid neighboring farms in search of an easy meal. It was not unheard of to come across a dog ravenously feeding on the carcass of a sloppily discarded animal. However, as a rule, dogs never seemed to raid their owner's farm. They went elsewhere. I remember, one day, when one of our neighbors shot and killed our black collie thinking that it was a wolf – so he told us later. Of course, we were none too happy as a dog was invaluable on a farm. But holding a grudge against one's neighbors could have serious consequences when help was later required.

Other years, when there wasn't an overabundance of predators, as luck would have it, it was their prey which thrived and wreaked havoc, this time with the farmers' crops. It was said that about every seven years or so the cycle of predator-prey went full circle. Rabbits, I recall, one year, had the upper hand, so to speak, and one fall and winter, they seemed to be everywhere enjoying a feeding frenzy on whatever they could find. In fact, one winter, you simply had to step outside the house at dusk or dawn and shoot into the pack without aiming and you would usually be guaranteed bag at least one each time. Over the next few years though, they would be seen less presumably having succumbed to starvation or disease as a result of their rapidly increasing numbers – only, of course, to have the cycle repeat itself several years later.

As well, when there was a shortage of foxes and coyotes, there quickly followed an infestation of small rodents such as mice and voles which could quickly and very easily eat up and destroy large amounts of cereal grain crops such as oats, wheat and barley on which farmers depended to feed their families as well as their cattle. Some years, even farmers' grain sheds in the winter became veritable havens for these rodents. Nothing seemed to be off limits to them. Even cats and poison could not keep up with eliminating them. And this combined with a near-annual summer invasion of grasshoppers, took its toll on farms. All a farmer could do then was to lick his wounds and take it on the chin, as it were, allowing, once again, the threat of starvation to poke its head around the corner. And so it was, what the elements didn't take away, the wildlife did.

Chapter 8 – Hunger Rears its Ugly Head

Hunger, I remember, was always a preoccupation while we were growing up. It was never life-threatening per se but it was chronic and all too real then. And, of course, since most farm families tended to be larger than the norm, this situation was bound never to improve itself unless measures were taken to fulfill the gastronomic needs of these families – and governments were certainly not in the habit of stepping in. By most standards, however, our family of nine members could even have been seen as relatively small compared to others. One of our more distant neighbors counted twenty-one members in his family and another had fifteen but generally seven or eight to ten or twelve was the norm for most farms - hence, the constant need to forage around or be on the lookout for food. Occasional hunting might have helped to alleviate the situation but prey was very difficult to get at - and very time consuming. Most farmers were just too busy looking after their own farms to pursue game around the countryside. And subsistence farming, as was practiced then, simply did not allow for the production of extra crops which could have been readily sold for much needed cash with which to buy food. Most of what was produced on the farm, except milk, was generally consumed by its own members, be they by the families themselves or their domestic livestock.

For many families, ours included, one way to relieve one's hunger was to follow in the footsteps of our ancestors of by-gone days and resort to the age-old method of gathering. Late summer and early fall was the time of year when wild berries would ripen giving us an opportunity to fill up our larder as well as our hollow stomachs. Every Sunday after Mass and a hasty lunch would see entire families head for the bush, each member with a pail in hand, ready to gather as many berries as they possibly could before nightfall. There was, most of the time, no dearth of berries providing one was willing to hike miles and miles of rough terrain over fallen branches and stumps in the bush for them. Some years, unfortunately, many of these berries had been all but wiped out by forest fires which often spontaneously erupted now and then. Such fires, however, did have a positive effect as they served to clear the underbrush and allow for a better production of berries the following year – providing new fires did not erupt. Unfortunately, it didn't do us much good during the year the fire spread unless it was before the berry-growing season. But, as usual, Mother Nature alone made that decision.

Anyway, while searching for these mouth-watering succulent little gems, you had, as well, to be always cognizant of the fact that you also had other competitors, not only humans but also animals. Bears, especially, were gorging themselves for their upcoming hibernation and were not too eager to share or part willingly with their bounty. Fortunately, going as groups, as we always did, made these predators a bit leery of challenging such a large number of noisy and boisterous humans. Of course, having our ever faithful canine companion to pinpoint one of these marauders before it came upon us was usually an added guarantee that we would not accidentally meet face to face..

After painstakingly and dutifully filling up our individual pails with a few choice leaves to make it appear fuller than they actually were, we would lay them down all together in a circle on the ground, guarded once again by man's best friend and proceed to fill our own stomachs sometimes to the point of over-gorging ourselves. Blueberries, strawberries and raspberries, which grow particularly well even in sandy soils, were usually plentiful in July and early August and these, of course, quickly became our preferred wild fruits. There were, as well, other berries which w called Saskatoons – blueberry-like fruits which grow higher up on branches - cranberries, pin cherries and, later in the season, choke cherries which we would sometimes pick and sell to passers-by who would use them to make home-made brew. This provided us with some of that much needed cash but hardly enough to make much of a difference in the family's cash flow problems. At other times, we would resort to scouring the neighborhoods in search of beer bottles left by townspeople who would go to the countryside on week-ends for their beer drinking parties. And jingling a few coins in our pockets gave us a sense of accomplishment. In fact, it may even have been a premonition of things to come.

Wild plants were another valuable source of food when berries were not readily available. Fireweeds and rosebuds, I recall, with their pretty reddish and pink flowers, were some of my specialties if I were brave enough to challenge the bees trying to pollinate them or use their nectar to make honey. Although we occasionally spotted their honeycombs, we wisely kept away from them after having been swarmed and stung a few times – we left that to the bears and other predators. However, these flowers were hardly enough to relieve our hunger. There were also the leaves of the giant blue hyssop which were particularly tasty – they had, I also recall, a distinctly licorice-like flavor which made them very attractive and appealing to our taste buds. There were, of course, many others as well. The only criterion at the time: if they were edible, we would gladly eat them. The way we saw it then was that if animals could survive on these plants, surely we could do no less. Even so, we were very lucky not to have poisoned ourselves in the process because I have later learned that not all plants edible to animals are also edible to humans – some are downright poisonous. There was only one plant that we stayed away from. Why, I don't know – maybe it was the smell. But it was very lucky for us that we did. That plant was none other than the mushroom.

Anyway, having finally filled ourselves with berries and temporarily satisfied our appetites, we were then ready to return home for the evening meal and the awaiting farm chores. It was then presumably not necessary to have a big meal thus leaving more food for the next day. Unfortunately, growing bodies, for some reason, always appear bottomless and any such savings quickly went down the hatch.

Year after year, however, it was this constant obsession with food which kept us going. But, in spite of this seemingly gloomy scenario there was, nevertheless, a positive aspect to this fact of life – a silver lining, if you will. None of us was destined to grow up obese – no, far from it. It was certainly not that we had planned it that way. Given a choice while growing up, things would certainly have been quite different. It is said though, and recent studies have also borne this out, that children who are overweight while very young tend to become overweight as adults. And, of course, the obverse is equally true. Children who are extremely slim while growing up – as all of us were, out of necessity – tend to remain that way as adults. It's probably due to the fact that such people do not have the habit of indulging so much in eating as their more overweight peers and it carries on with them throughout their adult lives – or maybe it could simply be due to the different rates of metabolism. Whatever the reasons, such appears to be a fact of life. But, of course, there is always a potential danger in such over-simplifications. In my case, when I was in Grade twelve and over six feet, my maximum weight was barely one hundred and forty pounds – a veritable beanpole – and I remained that way for quite some time afterwards. I have, of course, since gained more weight and even, at one time, reached two hundred and thirty pounds until my bout with cancer in later life.

Getting back to our food supply, we, like all farm families, of course had our garden plots but, as mentioned before, they were often fraught with problems. During these times, it would have been nice to have readily available cash to purchase at least the basic food necessities. But for a long time, that was out of the question, that is, until the youngest member of the family finally started school. Shortly after that, our mother was able to go out and look for work. And she found some – first, working in a sewing factory as some of our neighbors were doing – a veritable sweat shop in those days – and later, as a nurse's aide. Unfortunately, the latter position which she held until she passed away, was quite a distance from the farm – actually, it was in Otterburne - which meant that she would return home only on week-ends, and sometimes only every other week-end.

Now, with our Mom absent, everyone had to pitch in and take up the slack. That was when, I believe, we found out just how much work, all along, she had done for the entire family. But one fact was certain, if the family were to stay together, it now had to redouble its efforts and keep on struggling together. By that time, the second member of the family, my older sister was working on her own – so things were bound to get better. At least, there was some cash flowing in steadily for the first time – however small it might have been. Of course, Dad had done a few odd jobs outside the farm before but these had only been temporary and of short duration as he could not leave the farm for any prolonged period of time. Male heads of families were often forced to do that to help alleviate the financial burdens on the families – some worked in mines further north, others worked on pipelines even as far north as the Dew line as it was then called before it became obsolete as an early warning system for Russian bombers approaching North America from the Arctic while still others, like early 'coureurs de bois', headed for the bush either to cut lumber or set up traplines.

Unfortunately, in spite of her new job, our Mom still had plenty of work to do when she finally returned home. Eventually, the strain combined with her struggle with cancer proved too much for her to handle and she prematurely passed away at the age of fifty-four – a blow from which the family had difficulty coming to grips with. What was perhaps worst was that she was never able to witness the fate of her own children. In her final hours when she knew her demise was at hand, this was, no doubt, weighing heavily on her mind. Fortunately, most of us by then could reasonably be expected to look after ourselves if we had to.

Chapter 9 – A woman's work is never done

Farm Wife
She never climbed a mountain,
She never heard the sea,
But always watched a winding road
That wandered aimlessly
Among unshaded meadows –
A farm, a pasture, rife
With Black-eyed Susans, level fields
Comprised her little life.
She never longed to travel,
She felt no urge to search,
Her longest journey the six miles
On Sundays to the church;
Yet, in her quiet dwelling,
In singing, sighing flow,
Came love and parting, birth and death,
And all that women know.
John Hanlon Mitchell

While our lives revolved around a perpetual cycle of incessant toil for each and every member of the family, from the youngest to the oldest, no one bore a bigger and heavier burden than our own mother. And this was equally true of most farm women who were or would eventually become mothers themselves some day. For some, however, the burden of motherhood became too great and a few of them eventually entered Convents and became nuns – the so-called Brides of Christ – not that his was a less worthy profession but, no doubt, it created some friction between both groups as I have experienced directly while growing up. While nuns were generally respected and lauded for their spiritual roles in the community, their putative abdication of motherhood did not seem to sit well in certain circles. As a result, some of these women were shunned by certain members of the community. It was always a schoolyard practice to make fun of their habits and deplore the fact that, since they didn't have any children, they really didn't understand students. These leers also carried on in the adult world as well as I have heard many a housewife speak derisively – or was it enviously – of the old nuns. Whether or not that was simply maliciousness on the part of some people, these feelings were not just a whim. They were all too real.

But getting back to mothers, modern-day buzz words such as Super Mom, Marathon Mom and Multi-Tasking Moms are meant to show how busy modern-day housewives and mothers are, as if suddenly some authentic and original news has finally been imparted to the world and laid bare for all to see. Well, back then, while such terms were not yet in vogue, women were submitting themselves to such, and even harsher, practices as a common way of life. They didn't see it as anything unusual or special but as the necessary price to pay – although, I dare say, they probably even didn't see it as a price – for their lot in life. But, lest there be any confusion, farming women, I would even add, during these times, often paid inflated prices, as it were.

Our own mother, in spite of being everywhere, outside the house milking cows, cleaning the barn, feeding the chickens, putting up hay, caring for a fairly large garden and other chores, was also entrusted almost single-handedly with the tasks inside the home. Baking, cooking, preparing meals, sewing, cleaning the house, washing, drying and ironing the clothes – there was no permanent-press, then – making school lunches, to mention just a few, were part and parcel of her daily routine. And, not once, had she ever been heard to complain. I guess her deep and abiding faith in a higher power, combined with a love for her family, helped see her through even the hardest of times. This, it would appear, as mentioned before, was also the fate of many other farming housewives which, back then, was always graciously accepted, if not cheerfully, at least for the sake of their children. No wonder, some of them turned to ecclesiastical pursuits! How, we may very well ask nowadays, these housewives could cope with such seemingly superhuman burdens is really fantastic in itself. Certainly present-day hardworking women had role-models then. In fact, the role of the pioneer housewife has been so neglected by modern historians that few people are aware of their contributions to the development of early communities.

Every Saturday, after a heavy work-week, our mother could be seen busily engaged, among other chores, in doing the laundry for the whole family. And this was after a few hours working in the barn, making breakfast and washing the dishes. When I was younger, I even still have a faint recollection of watching her washing clothes on a washboard on her hands and knees by a little creek which flowed across our farm scrubbing for hours until each item was suitably cleaned. Later, when we got electricity, she was fortunate enough to acquire a used old wringer washing machine with twin rollers between which she would lovingly pass each item of clothing to squeeze out as much water and soap as possible. Then, as I watched in a semi-detached state, she would take them outside to hang on the clothes lines and wait for them to dry praying that it wouldn't rain. One week's dirty clothes would generally take Mom the whole of Saturday to wash and sometimes well into Sunday morning, all the while, stopping to make lunch and dinner. Then, in the evening, she would be ready to go to the barn again.

Later, after the grueling tasks of washing and drying the clothes were over came the ironing. And, of course, there was usually a practically insurmountable mound of clothes to tackle. And, before we were fortunate enough to have electricity, the only way to heat up an iron was to put it on a hot stove. Imagine ironing beside a burning stove in the middle of summer! Sometimes, the stove got too hot and the iron had to be gauged just right or the clothes would be seared. Of course, it was not unheard of to wear a piece of clothing which had had a close encounter with a red-hot iron. And as if that were not enough, there was still sewing to do. I still remember the constant whizzing sound of her old Singer sewing machine as it stitched torn or worn-out clothing. In addition, since there was no cash to buy new clothing, most of them had to be sewn at home from scratch or by re-sewing hand-me-downs. The hours she spent in front of that sewing machine, day and night, were testimony to the care and devotion with which she looked after the family.

If any praise was to be heaped on any class of people of that era, it certainly must be heaped generously on the farming women of these frontier societies. It is not to say that the burden for the modern-day woman is any less difficult to bear. But, whereas, there are more avenues for help and support more readily available now, they were largely non-existent then. Often, farm women then had very little recourse but to grin and bear it, as it were. Over the years, I often wondered if our own mother had ever entertained dreams of an easier life. And who could have blamed her? Certainly, she never even hinted or gave any indication of them. How she was able to cope with the fate which was bestowed upon her was, I would say, a bit beyond comprehension.

I remember of one very hot summer day when she was out in the field, pitchfork in hand, piling hay. At the time, I was sitting in the shade of a haystack chewing on a strand of hay and watching my mother work when, all of a sudden, she fell limp to the ground – perhaps a premonition of worst to come later in life. She had just had a heat stroke. I yelled to my father who immediately rushed to her side. After a few minutes in the shade and a bit of water, she seemed to have regained her faculties and was able to resume her work as if nothing had happened. Now, that was internal fortitude at its height! At that time, however, I had not realized the gravity of what had just taken place. It was only several years later when I recalled that incident that it hit me. My own mother could easily have expired at that moment right in front of my very eyes. Heat strokes, I was told, have sometimes proved fatal. I still often wonder if, in fact, I could have shouldered that burden at such a tender age for the rest of my life. But, worse yet, what would have happened to the family if she had passed away then? Could our Dad have shouldered the whole load by himself?

Fathers, of course also, had it very difficult then. The mere burden as head of the household of assuring that the family could successfully eke out a living, however, meager, on the land must have weighed heavily on their shoulders, as well. They were, after all, then, seen as the main bread winners and any failure to support their families would indeed have been a harsh punishment to take and perhaps even interpreted as a sign of their weakness in spirit on their part. That was why, for some, abandoning the land, in the end, seemed to be the only alternative left if their families were to have any chance of surviving intact. But while such decisions were often the province of the fathers, it was the mothers who carried the heavier burden, it would seem, since, then as now, they had a seemingly greater stake in the fortunes of their own children. This, it would appear, has always been a fact of nature – be it with humans or in the animal world.

Bearing and rearing seven children almost single-handedly, as my mother had done, was in itself truly remarkable and inspiring, especially given the very primitive conditions of the time. Every fever, stomach upset or headache had to be looked after by her even to the yanking out of our very first baby teeth. Nowadays, we often hear complaints of parents having to raise two or three children while surrounded with all the medical technology and expertise of the day. It is necessary only, during these times, to stop and reflect for a while on the not-too-distant past and imagine ourselves in these primitive situations and living under these, often very appalling, conditions. Eventually we would undoubtedly come to the realization that our own lot in life is not so bad after all. And it is, in large part, due to the dedication and pioneering spirit of these largely forgotten women of the past who have almost single-handedly raised large families, many, whose members have gone on to become prosperous and productive members of society.

Chapter 10 – The Patriarch of the Family

Small in stature,
Eyes bay blue,
And as deep;
Lower jaw like a cliff,
Tongue silent,
As hard and strong as a husky.
Adapted from E.J. Pratt

At a height of slightly over five feet three inches, he could hardly be said to have been an imposing figure. Yet, our Dad was that and more. While his physical stature was less than impressive, he was easily able to command respect not only from his family but also from those around him simply by disarming them with his penetrating eyes. His outlook and disposition were generally pleasant and even-handed, but these belied the fact that he could be abrasive at times if need be. When in a foul mood although usually a man of few words, he was not one to be easily trifled with as witnessed occasionally by the odd family member or neighbor who had had the misfortune of earning his wrath.

Raised in a harsh frontier environment where his own father would not hesitate to cuff him around the head on occasions, it was only natural that he would reciprocate in kind with his own family. However, his administration of justice was still a very far cry from his own experiences growing up. He had, of course, as he told us later, always done his best to make sure that the kind of strict country discipline which he had met at the hands of his own father would not be revisited upon us. Unfortunately, this was not always the case.

I remember the times when we would be chased around the yard with my Dad holding a well-knotted piece of rope in one hand and uttering a few choice expletives in the process. It was during these times that you really found out just how fast you could run. At other times, the shiny brown 3-inch wide, ¼-inch thick, 3-feet long leather belt with which he used to sharpen his razor would serve just fine on short notice. A few well-placed flings of that steroid-laden fly swatter and the party was pretty well over. Of course, looking back on it now, being the sometimes combative rabble rousing siblings that we were and eager to take on dares, we probably brought on some of these bouts of fury on his part. And, forbearance and patience were generally not virtues practiced then. Fortunately, for us, such country-style justice tended to be very infrequent and generally accepted as the norm then. As the saying went: everyone did it. This brand of justice, at the time, was as natural as hay rides in the winter or doing farm chores – they came as part of the package, as it were.

But discipline was only part of the responsibilities of heads of families then, as now – except that nowadays they tend to be shared more equally by both parents. However, as they say, first you must gain the attention of the mule and only then will it do your bidding. I guess, some of us were perhaps a bit mule-headed thus forcing certain extreme measures in order to get our attention. And it generally fell to the male heads of families to make sure that everyone towed the line. Fathers had to make sure that the homestead would endure and provide a reasonable source of living for its members. This was a colossal task as every year, with new mouths to feed, farm resources became taxed to their limit and constant work and vigilance by everyone were needed just to keep the farm viable.

Every season saw my Dad scurrying around, whether in the searing heat of a mid-summer sun or the bone-chilling cold of frigid winters, to provide for the rest of us. And, as cash was out of the question then, new and inventive ways had to be devised to keep everyone afloat as going to the corner store was simply not an option. But simply to note that there was always an abundance of farm chores to perform would minimize the hardships incurred by their execution. To get the proper perspective and feel the impact of the types of chores that were then necessary for farms to survive, it is necessary to outline some of them.

In particular, I recall how Dad would, every summer, labor long and hard just to put fences around our farm to keep our animals in. This would entail hours and hours of back-breaking work as the sheer number of pickets, or posts, which he had to saw to length and sharpen, then put in the ground, numbered in the hundreds. And, every year, many got broken either by animals or by the sheer force of heavy winds or simply as a result of rotting. These, then, had to be pulled out individually and replaced, one by one, all by hand. As we got older, we provided some help.

But for a long time, he was on his own. I can still picture him, a little man loading a huge wagon, with the apparent ease, strength and dexterity of one twice his size, with dozens of heavy wooden posts and heading out to the fields to set them in. And, this was just part of the task required. He had then to affix a double barbed-wire fence around the entire line of pickets. In spite of wearing gloves and heavy overalls, his many severe cuts, scrapes and bruises were witness to the hazards of the job. And once this was completed, he would then attach an electric device to electrify the entire fence. In this way, would-be predators or scavengers would also hopefully be dissuaded from entering the farmstead. Unfortunately, there were always ways around it.

As well, in the summer heat, I remember him spending hour upon hour unloading and stacking loose hay in the loft beside the barn with only a pitchfork and the sheer determination that went with it as sweat constantly poured down his forehead. He would simply wipe the accumulated sweat off his brow, blow his nose then continue on. And when one load had been unloaded, he would quickly head back to the field for another one – oftentimes without even stopping at the house for a break. The hay had to be brought in before winter set in and there was little time to waste – especially since this was largely a one-man task until we were old enough to help.

During winters as well, Dad would not hesitate to pit himself against the rigors of the cold even in the wee hours of the morning. I particularly remember the trouble he had to go to just to ensure that our milk was delivered on time every day. While we generally had a milk truck coming to our farm to pick up the milk, there were many times in winter when the roads became impassable and the truck couldn't make it to the farm. It was during these times that Dad had devised a plan where he would cross through our neighbor's field and deliver the milk to the main road which could then be picked up by the milk truck. For this, he had to get up around 4:00 am or earlier, harness a horse onto a sleigh and proceed in the dark loaded with the milk cans from the previous day. The trip, one-way, was over a mile – not a particularly daunting task if you are in the middle of summer. But in knee-deep snow with temperatures hovering around minus 30 degrees with a possible wind chill factor in the low 50s, things become a bit different. But this was just the beginning. When he had reached the end of the road, he often had to wait extended periods of time for the truck to arrive – all the while hoping that he had not missed it and be forced to return home with his milk still on board.

While he and our neighbor both had to undertake this trek, they had hastily built a makeshift cabin with a small window facing the road and equipped it with a small pot-bellied stove with which to warm themselves while waiting for the truck. During such times, you had to be resourceful as well as industrious, if you wanted to survive the wrath of the elements.

As well, in the winters, I remember Dad taking out his ax and saw and heading into the forest to try and cut down as many trees as possible as there never seemed to be enough time in the fall after harvest to supply all the wood needed for burning throughout the year. To get there, he would have to walk through deep snows, then, before cutting each tree, he would have to dig the snow around it – a very time-consuming job. I remember one time when he returned home after a long walk through the snow bleeding profusely from a severed toe. Apparently, the deep snow had confused his aim and he had brought the ax down on his foot cutting part of his big toe. He had simply walked home - I'm sure in excruciating pain - through the deep snow then, upon arrival, removed his boot and blood-soaked socks, cleaned the wound, bandaged it up then returned to resume his wood cutting. He was that type of a man, a true hardy and tough frontiersman. There was no denying that. Lesser men, myself included, would have been bed-ridden for days complaining about the pain, but not him. A small man though he may have been, he more than made up for it in his prowess, zeal and determination to get the job done.

This is not to say though that all farmers were necessarily forced to adopt such measures but, owing to our situation, extreme isolation and distance from other farms, we had little choice. Outside help was simply not an option, especially in winters. For Dad, however, in spite of the nature of the work, it was probably only a continuation of what he had been used to when he was just a young man living on his father's farm. Back then, as he later recounted, he and other young men would travel dozens of miles in mid-winter through heavy bush country, in deep snows, with a sleigh and a team of horses to get at the timber stands suitable to harvest and cart back to their farmsteads – or to whomever had hired their services at the time. They would, he told me, often have to traverse several small towns in the process to reach the area where the suitable timber stands were located. I remember the place names he had mentioned – Bedford, Marchand, Sprague, Piney among others. I have visited all these places in the comfort of an automobile but to think that they had actually been reached – and by-passed - from his family farm in Otterburne by horse and sleigh, and in the middle of winter not only brings into reality the vast distances these sylvan 'voyageurs' had to travel but the sheer mental and physical energy they had to expend in doing so.

I often wonder if I would have had the dedication, perseverance or the will to undertake what my own father had in the past. It is one thing to glory in this past while sitting comfortably in the confines of your living-room but that was reality then – in its most brazen and rugged sense. While other male heads of families, veritable patriarchs in their own right, no doubt, had similar experiences to recount, they too must be saluted, very much as we salute our own heroes of today, for their substantial contributions to the development of our frontier societies.

Chapter 11 – For whom the bell tows

O Lord, who can unroll Thy mysteries?
For Thou hast made in the Height chambers
For some are treasures of salvation,
And some are treasures of fire,
And rivers of brimstone,
For the breakers of the covenant.
Adapted from Solomon ibn Gabriol

Spiritual guidance has always been sought by countless people ever since the dawn of civilization or even before judging from the recently discovered burial sites left by the so-called Neanderthal Man living in Europe about fifty thousand years ago. When these first primitive religious urgings had their humble beginnings, no one really knows for sure. In any case, it is a moot point since people everywhere, in order to cope with the supernatural forces of nature and help ease their daily burdens, have always counted on a closer relationship with their Creator whether he himself was a human creation as some skeptics have argued or has always existed since time immemorial. What is known, however, is that out of these first stirrings grew the world's great religions of today. And, of course, the most ardent adherents and believers of these religions have always tended to be the poor, the unfortunate and the downtrodden, as it were, of the world. Religions, among other things, offered them – and still do – a sort of mechanism by which to escape the monotony, drudgery and apparent meaninglessness of their daily lives and encourage them to dream of a better one of joy, happiness and fulfillment to come. And, certainly, this is no less true for tens of millions of people today as it was during any period in the past.

In the little hamlet of LaBroquerie where I was raised, the Church had always been the centerpiece, even the pinnacle, of all activities – from offering daily Mass services to bingos - and, as such, had always, from its very inception, figured very prominently in the day-to-day lives of its parishioners. Not one day ever went by that there wasn't any number of people inside asking either forgiveness for their sins, seeking divine intervention in their lives or simply offering prayers for their departed loved ones. Every Sunday and holy days, in addition, would always witness the arrival, en masse, of the greater part, by far, of the population which surrounded it, as well as many others from far and wide. All possible attempts were made to attend at least every Sunday mass because failing to do so would, it was widely believed and reinforced by the local clergy, bring down certain unbearable consequences from above – fire and brimstone being the main ingredients. And this combined with the meager conditions of one's lifestyle, was more grief than anyone wanted to bear. As a result, everyone who could possibly make it to church – either by buggy, on horseback, sleigh or simply hiking – made it. Certainly our family was also one of them.

Not every parishioner, though, who attended church was necessarily destitute but these tended to be in the minority. Attendance at Mass, in essence, in addition to providing spiritual cleansing to its adherents also provided a forum for everyone to get re-acquainted and share information about the latest developments in the lives of its inhabitants. And, of course, it was on Sundays that important news was imparted to the community by the local priest as it was the only day of the week when most of the parishioners were congregated under one roof.

So every Sunday would see us harness the horses to a buggy or a sleigh and, with the whole family packed in it, travel the six or so miles to Church. In later years, of course, with the arrival of a used car, the trip became a bit more enjoyable. However, in the deep winter snows and freezing weather, it was still necessary to bundle up and get the horses and sleigh out. Mom, especially, would never even think of not attending Mass even in the dead of winter – even if we had to walk. Fortunately, to my recollection, it never came to that.

Once in church, I still recall vividly, at the entrance of the big wooden square doors, how we would immediately genuflect and make the symbolic sign of the cross with anointed water from a basin left there for that purpose then slowly make our way upstairs to our assigned pews. Downstairs was generally reserved for those who could afford to rent them – which, of course, left us out, only to stare at them curiously as we headed up the stairs. Anyway, whether to justify my lot, or otherwise, I had convinced myself that I preferred the upstairs pews as they were closer to the church organ and choir. And what a choir! I remember how I would often look back and listen single-mindedly half-smitten with incredulity and amazement at the magnificent and enticing sounds coming out of both the organ and the staccato, resonating voices of the male members of the choir. I suspect that, at that time, a lot of other churchgoers also attended church in part to listen to the choir which seemed to possess some magic power capable of elevating your spirits to unfathomable heights of sheer delight and ecstasy. Anyway, they were a welcome diversion from the dry, humorless homilies delivered by the priest. But how this little wilderness village could produce such mesmerizing music – certainly it was a far cry from the incessant creaking of old machinery back on the farm – and singing was truly miraculous. This, no doubt contributed, at least in part, to the heightened aura of religious fervor among the parishioners.

About half way through the ceremony, it was always the custom to pass around a collection plate for donations. I remember how Mom would always frantically look around the house for any loose change before leaving home to make sure she always had a few pennies to donate. Being highly religious, she believed that a higher power from above would never forgive her for her sins of omission if she failed in her weekly donation to the Church. Dad, of course, was a bit more lackadaisical in his beliefs and it never seemed to bother him as much – at least not outwardly. In any case, I still remember that bright, shiny silver collection platter laden with large bills inside which made our meager contributions pale in comparison. I really think that Mom would purposely lay down the coins gently so as not to make any noise to make it appear as if we also had donated some bills. And, of course for us, these few pennies often meant the difference between a new pair of shoes or old hand-me-downs or even an extra sandwich for school. But that was the price we had to pay, I thought at the time, for a belief in some form of salvation in the next world. Anything to alleviate our suffering on this earth and the promise of better things to come quickly made us forget these new shoes – or that extra slice of bread.

Once mass was over, I would marvel at the throngs of parishioners who would swarm out of church only to congregate at the entrance doorway blocking the way for lingering church-goers who were a bit slow on the take-of. However, it was then and there that a lot of the community business was conducted and disputes resolved. With a priest standing in their midst, ready to call down the forces from above, it was very unlikely that heated arguments would ever take place – with the end result being that most inhabitants would return home in good spirits, or, at least, giving that impression. And, the next time that most of them would get a chance to meet would again be at that same front entrance to the Church under a gleaming spire and presumably also under the ever watchful eye of their Creator. In addition, it was also the practice then – which has now largely been abandoned in many communities – for the parish priest to visit each parishioner at least once a year. This way, any wayward inhabitant could be reined in, if necessary – thus further reinforcing the tight grip the church exercised over its flock.

Such a pivoting role, of course, was deemed necessary by the church in pioneering communities to reassure the inhabitants that their souls would be looked after in the other world as well as in this one. Nowadays, such a role has become more symbolic than real. In fact, to the disparagement of some, the role the Church once played in the lives of its parishioners has now diminished greatly as there are now less needy people who rely on its succor as they once did. As well, the increased pace of life has left the Church, in large part, trying to find new and creative ways to re-connect with its parishioners. And, of course, with people gradually becoming better off and more worldly, the trappings of religion, as they have always been presented, and all their implications have become less important in their daily lives – as it has in ours, as well.

However, there is no denying the central role religion had played in our daily lives. I still recall vividly, every evening at home, every member of the family would kneel down, with our mother sitting in her favorite chair, to recite the evening prayers, oftentimes, for us kids, only uttering these prayers in a semi-detached mood wishing for the merciful arrival of the end. Anyway, these prayers were another instance of families sharing some time together thus strengthening the bonds that would later hold them together - and enabling them to struggle with all that life threw their way.

Chapter 12 – Beckoning New Trails

As children, and perhaps quite understandably so, during our earlier years at least, we were never really fully cognizant of the squalor of our existence as all our neighbors as well, at least those within close proximity to us, were living under very similar conditions. At school, we met other children who also shared in our way of life and as far as we knew, everyone in our little universe lived that way. And life as we had come to know it continued unabated, that is, until we were forced to change school. Up until then, the little one-room school house had been all that we knew about schooling. We had loved it, even cherished it, especially when combined with the camaraderie of other like-minded classmates and the close, enduring, steadfast bonds we had developed with them over the years – our Huckleberry Finn years, I would later call them. At recesses, we could not wait to go out there with our classmates and hunt for these ever-elusive four-legged little invaders, the ground squirrels. I shall never forget these days as they, too, have become indelibly imprinted in my memory to this day – happy moments, they certainly were! Climbing trees was another of our favorite pastimes as was building 'forts' out of old dead, decaying and dry branches pretending all along that we were cowboys and Indians. Back then, we felt a real sense of permanency about our way of life and believed that it would always remain that way. Even books were not high on our agenda, if they were even on our radar screens at all. Yes, as the saying goes, those were the days my friend. However, when I entered grade six, all this gradually began to change.

The new school building, located, as it was, right in the center of town very close to the Church, in fact, separated only by a nuns' Convent, was an immense brown stucco structure with large entrance doors – and two side entrances - presumably to accommodate the larger number of students. It had two levels with a staircase leading to. Imagine that, a second floor. That had certainly impressed me then. It even boasted a library of sorts – but no gymnasium, as I recall – something which, of course, was foreign to us new kids. And there were students everywhere! And so many classrooms!

I still remember the first day I arrived there. I was standing in the school yard and, for the first time, I was surrounded by what seemed to be throngs of laughing, giggling and boisterous students, the likes of which I had never experienced before, certainly, not on such a grandiose scale. Farming folks, at least then, tended to be much more docile, more introspect and generally less given to frivolous and loud chatter – except perhaps in small groups. Certainly we perceived ourselves that way. It was a bit scary and unnerving for me. I remember feeling my insides begin to seize and tense up at the sight of so many people. It didn't help matters that I didn't recognize anyone as our family, at the time, had been among the first ones to leave the shelter of our little school house that year. In time, however, other families were soon to follow.

That day, when the school bell rang, everyone raced to the school entrance to line up in their assigned rows according to grades. Suddenly a new kind of crippling fear gripped me. Where was the sixth-grade class? I furtively and anxiously looked around trying to see if somehow I could spot a clue that would signal where my new classmates might be. Unfortunately, I couldn't find any. It was then that a matronly elderly teacher, the traditional portrait of a real-life school marm - mother and teacher types bundled into one – approached me quietly and a bit inquisitively and asked me what grade I was in, then politely directed me in the right direction. That was my first panic attack, but it would not be my last, as I was to find out later.

It wasn't long, however, before I started to fit in – as did my siblings in the other classrooms. The only problem was that here, for the very first time, we finally came face to face with the stark realization that indeed there were other more fortunate students who appeared to be better clothed, better fed and seemed to have coins always jingling in their pockets. Slowly, as time passed, we could perceive a sense of us and them – something which had previously been alien to us. It was not simply that they were townspeople and we were country yeomen, as it were - common people living off the land. It was partly that. But there was also a much more subtle difference. As well as being better off than we were, they also appeared more refined in their tastes, perhaps a bit more sophisticated and world-wise. In fact, I remember my amazement and astonishment when I first saw and listened to one of my new town classmates actually playing the piano. I don't remember the tune but it sounded great to me at the time. How I wished I could have played or joined in too. Trying not to appear too conspicuous, I slowly inched myself closer to get a better look. In my little world, such people only lived in a little black box called a radio – or at Church.

It was then, I believe, that new and exciting ideas started to germinate and percolate in our young growing minds. Certainly, they did in mine. Maybe, just maybe, life on the farm, as we knew it, was not all there was. Maybe there was something else out there waiting for us. In fact, we were slowly learning one of life's little quirks. People generally tend to be satisfied with their lot in life as long as it is shared with all those around them and that is all they are aware of at the time. However, as soon as it is realized or known, even perceived, that different and more exciting lifestyles exist, everyone wants to share in them. As we didn't even own a television set at the time, life on the farm had been an acceptable way of life to be endured in spite of its dreariness and constant toil. Ignorance indeed, was bliss. But now that other lifestyles were not only known to exist but were actually deemed to be possibly attainable, our whole outlook on life slowly began to take on a different turn.

All of a sudden, farm work became more of a burden which had to be tolerated to survive instead of it being wedded to our collective psyches as it had always been. Work on the farm now became more of a means for survival rather than an intrinsic desire in itself to make a success of the farm. Whereas earlier we had always intended to labor on as sod-busters, as it were, throughout our adult lives, our thoughts now gradually gravitated elsewhere. For the first time, we started to dream of another life, perhaps one even far removed from this little piece of land we had called our own and had, until then, become so fond of.

Such world shattering realizations, of course, do not manifest themselves in a short span of time and without some consequences. The little farm, no matter how miserable it might have appeared to outsiders, was still our home and refuge and that feeling would remain with us for a very long time. What did develop, however, was a sort of tug-of-war in our own minds which practically tore us apart. On the one hand, it seemed blasphemous, even sacrilegious to even contemplate the idea of turning our backs on our past and abandoning the kind of life our parents had stoically endured and had half-expected us to follow. It had always been the practice in the past that the children would inherit and expand the family farms. So, for a long time, we simply chose to ignore the possibility of a better life and dutifully accepted our lot and continued to toil on the farm. But the seeds of change had been sown and there was to be no turning back – a new trail was beckoning.

Unbeknownst to us at the time, we inadvertently started to bury our heads more deeply into our books, probably mimicking our new school mates and redoubling our efforts to succeed in the classroom - in other words, from hunting squirrels to hunting for new words. This may have been the direct result of larger classrooms which encouraged us to excel even more or it may have been due to the fact that our somewhat previously narrow-minded attitudes toward books were slowly being supplanted by a healthier and more mature approach toward learning for its own sake. Whatever it was, there definitely was evidence of a sort of disaffection with our lot in life gradually creeping up in our collective subconscious.

Eventually, the path became clearer and a new road was revealing itself on the horizon. Whether we chose to struggle and complete grade school or decided to leave earlier, the bug had bitten us and a better life than could be offered on the farm was in our direct line of vision. From then on, our efforts became directed toward the realization of such a lifestyle. Unfortunately, my older brother and sister were not able to partake in this transition as they had already been forced to leave school at relatively young ages to follow their own dreams which, initially did not appear too promising and invariably would take them away from the halls of academia where, for the rest of us, the trail was leading. Essentially, we had finally arrived at the edge of a symbolic precipice and had to make a decision – to jump in the abyss or risk it all on the edge and watch the world go by. In the end, we decided, like Thelma and Louise, to throw caution to the wind and take the plunge.

The psychological effects alone, however, had to be reckoned with before we set our sights on this new way of life – this brave new world, to borrow a term from Aldous Huxley. We had to make it clear in our own minds that we were ready and willing to submerge our past and all it stood for and embrace a future, however uncertain, which promised the kind of success we could barely envision at the time, as well as enlightenment to guide us on our path. Farm life had been a certainty. You knew exactly what to do to succeed although that success undoubtedly came at a very heavy price but it was one which could be understood and taken into account. Away from the farm, however, uncertainty would become the new buzz word, uncertainty about how to approach this new lifestyle to make it a success, albeit a success no more guaranteed than on the farm. All this had to be thoroughly explored in our own minds before a final decision could be taken. No wonder then that such a final decision, for each one of us, could not be taken until shortly before leaving school. As for me, even as I set out on my new path after High School, I felt pangs of remorse and longings for leaving the family farm which subsisted long after I had left it.

One unfortunate event, however, took place which helped somewhat to loosen the strings attached to our way of life. It was our own mother's untimely demise. Ever since we were born, she had always been there for us and, in a sense, personified all that was good and pure about this land. She had been everywhere on the farm. Now that she was gone, there seemed to be less reason to hold on to our past. Not that we would ever forget it. That was definitely not going to happen. It was only that now we fully realized that this past was not as permanently engraved in our psyches or etched in stone as we had once believed. Also, as if an added impetus, the idea of leaving the farm had also become a factor in the decisions of our peers at the time. And the more we discussed it, the more we came to the conclusion that this was the right path to follow.

I remember that not very long after moving to the larger school in town, for the first time, we started discussing the types of professions we would like to go in much to the chagrin and consternation of our baffled parents who had not counted on our eventual alienation from this little farmstead. However, realizing the appalling conditions we had been subjected to while growing up, they eventually relented and realized that perhaps life in the outside world would probably hold more promise than lingering on the farm in the hopes that some day it would miraculously become a sort of oasis in this vast desolate wilderness of largely wind-swept sand and rocks. In my own case, it had been expected that I would go into the priesthood thus tying me indirectly to the land by ministering to the parishioners. Over time, however, slowly and begrudgingly at first, our parents were to come on board, although I know with heavy hearts, and even started to suggest avenues we could explore for our future. But before we had settled on any one profession, in our now confused minds, we had to go through a whole myriad of them seemingly trying them out before making a final decision – a decision though that would be entirely of our own choosing. So rightly or wrongly, the consequences would not only be for each one of us to endure but also our own responsibility. The question was: would leaving the farm be the correct choice? Only time would tell.

Chapter 13 – After the plunge

How cold, still and lonely, how weary you seem!
A last wistful look and I'll go.
Oh, will you remember the lad with his dream!
The lad that you comforted so.
The shadows enfold you, it's drawing to-night,
The evening star needles the sky;
And huh! But it's stinging and stabbing my sight
God bless you, old cabin, good-bye!
Robert Service

Shortly after our mother had passed away, the farm was finally sold to a neighbor for a very paltry sum, even at that time. He had wanted to enlarge his own farmstead but, as everyone was then, he was short on cash and collateral. And since his was the only semi-reasonable offer we had had, we had reluctantly decided to let it go – a whole life of blood, sweat and tears for barely a fistful of dollars! It hardly seemed worth it. But since none of us had really wanted to continue living on it, letting it go even at that price seemed to provide us with a sense of relief for the constant toil we had put into it. And now, more so with our mother gone, we felt it was best to let sleeping dogs lie, as it were. Even Tiger had passed on, the unfortunate victim of a hit and run by an automobile, no less. I remember when I first saw her lying inertly on the road not too far from our house. Her entrails were slowly oozing out of her mouth – such had been the force of the blow with which she had been struck – as she lay there motionless and lifeless. It was the last we ever saw of her. She was quickly buried next to her predecessor. Yes, maybe it was best after all to let go of the past and embrace a new future, a future that would hopefully be brighter for the rest of us.

Our father, now appearing frail and somewhat disoriented over the recent loss of his beloved wife, soon moved in a little bungalow downtown where, for the first time in a very long while, he worked for someone else. He had always said that he loved the farm as he could be his own boss there. No doubt, this turn of events was a blow to his now sagging spirit. He hired himself out as a milk quality control officer where he would go from farm to farm and test the milk – a position which he fortunately felt comfortable with. He would work at that, combined with a few other odd jobs, until his retirement when he would move again, for the final time, to the city. For him, this last move, undoubtedly would have felt like a severe culture shock as he had never cared for city life much less live in one. However, he was destined to remaine there until his own demise several years later and, although he never directly told anyone, of a broken heart feeling that his entire life had produced so little wealth but had entailed so many hardships and toil for his entire family in the process. It had always been his ardent wish to give his family more than he had received when he was growing up but, unfortunately, it was not to be. I sometimes wondered, however, if, during this time, he had ever asked himself if he had made the right decision so many years ago to raise a family in what was then a rugged, wild, semi-arid ecosystem in Southern Manitoba rather than moving with our mother to the huge plains of Saskatchewan – albeit just as dry and uninviting at the time.

The rest of us, on the other hand, went on to various professions and, in the end, all fared reasonably well. My eldest brother became successful in the trucking business, eventually owning and operating his own rig, while my eldest sister fared equally well in the restaurant sector. As for the twins and I, we eventually found our way in the field of education where we became successful educators. For my part, I first spent about eight years in the wilderness of Northern Manitoba – perhaps the consequences of my earlier life on the farm or the result of unresolved issues – trying various jobs before returning to the halls of academia and finally becoming a public school teacher. My youngest brother – he with the unique tuft of white hair in the middle of light brown hair – went into the auto body business where he built up a successful career for himself and his family. As for my youngest sister, she went to work for the federal government eventually carving out a successful and lucrative niche for herself and her family in that field.

Over the years, unable to completely abandon the past, we would often go and visit what used to be our home even pretending that it still was – certainly it remained in our hearts and minds. Needless to say, it saddened us to see that the buildings, the house, the barn, the sheds as well as the farm machinery – which had now become either too old or obsolete – were left unattended and allowed to crumble and decay to be gradually engulfed by weeds. I really believe, when I was last there, that these weeds were eyeing me gleefully as if saying: Ha! Ha! We won! We won! Anyway, while there, we would always walk through what used to be our yard and garden, reflect on the spot, take a few fleeting glances around, especially in the direction of the oak tree in the distance – or what was left of it – check out the rapidly dilapidating buildings, all the while secretly shedding a few tears and wondering if we had, in fact, made the right decision by abandoning our old homestead. Leaving one's childhood home is always very difficult and perhaps even more so for us as this was the only way of life we had ever known and, in some way, cherished in spite of its many hardships, while growing up. Farm life, in a sense, had insulated us from the outside world. Other lifestyles had always appeared distant and cold to us – even after the plunge. Nevertheless, in spite of our continued tormented feelings and lingering doubts about leaving, in the end, we had to contend with the fact that our decision had already been taken, the farm was sold and that we had to live with it.

In fact, it was actually sealed permanently and irrevocably for us when, for the last time, we decided to go back once again to pay our respects to our old home. To our chagrin and utter despair, everything, all the buildings, even the house, had been completely bulldozed, razed to the ground, and it had become virtually impossible to identify the exact location of our old farm buildings – even the old oak tree had finally been completely uprooted – a once proud denizen in the landscape. I guess what the tornado had been unable to finish, men had. That sight, even more than any other, touched us the most. With that tree completely gone, so was any reason to come back. In fact, our link to that past had now been irrevocably severed. It was then that, although we still did not want to admit it out loud, we finally realized it was definitely time to let go. There was nothing more to gain by coming back – except pain and agony. However, it did take all the courage we could muster to stop from heading in that direction whenever we happened to be in the vicinity – although, I have to admit, we did secretly.

But now that every trace of our ever having lived there had disappeared, even the memories were slowly fading away. Fortunately, we still had black and white pictures to hold on to – largely the products of an old box camera which had served us well over the years – which we often take out to reminisce. These and fading memories are now all that we have left as witness that we had once lived there. Nevertheless, it still feels a bit eerie to acknowledge that a family which had once worked, played and prayed there was now no more — a mere footnote, if even that, of history. This, perhaps as much as anything else, has made us realize the transient nature of all things earthly. As the old saying goes: here one day, gone tomorrow. That, I guess, is the moral we have to take with us as we continue to make our way in this world. However, in real life, it is never quite that simple or easy to internalize. But, as they say, as one door closes another one opens.

Chapter 14 – Brave New Worlds

As each one of us left the farm, it was with great anticipation and certainly some degree of apprehension as to what would be in store for us out there. We were, after all, casting our nets in uncharted waters and the great unknown beyond. Farm life had not really prepared any of us for this new world now facing us although it had provided us with at least one valuable tool, one which would remain with us for the rest of our lives – a positive work ethic combined with a sense that anything was possible if you wanted it badly enough. It had shown us the intrinsic value of hard work and, as such, made us realize that only with diligence, persistence, a bit of sweat, and, of course, a whole lot of good luck would we be able to compete and succeed in the outside world – a world, however, in which we would have to begin exploring with small, cautious steps.

Although none of us could have predicted with any degree of certainty at the time what lay ahead in our separate paths, we all greeted this new world, these new horizons, if you will, with outstretched arms and the innocent glee of young children. There was no denying that when we left the farm we were relative greenhorns in search of more worldly pastures. We were virtually on our own now and gradually setting our sights on new vistas. And where these avenues would eventually lead us, only God Almighty could know for sure – and He certainly wasn't talking. But one thing was certain, a whole new life was opening itself up at our very feet and the onus was now on us to make use of the opportunity given to us. We had to grab that proverbial bull by the horns and try to hang on. Falling off simply would not be an option.

For my part, initially, I found it somewhat difficult to adjust to this new life. Not really knowing what line of work to throw myself into, for several years I gravitated in Northern Manitoba perhaps a bit aimlessly from one job to another never really feeling comfortable or at ease with any one of them – from teaching to mining to hotel work to general labor. Luckily, at the time, jobs were not too difficult to come by and I never experienced any impediments moving from one to another – except for my last one. Suddenly, as a direct result of increased immigration, it seemed that there were now a lot more applicants for far fewer jobs

– especially if you didn't possess any special skills. It was then that I decided it might be a good idea to go to University and train myself for a profession. Interestingly enough, I soon found out that I rather enjoyed this new direction my life was now taking and so continued on for several years all the while acquiring my credentials to become an educator – the very first job I had taken temporarily when I left the farm. I guess what goes around comes around.

My first full-time teaching assignment was my most difficult, as is normal in any profession – but it proved to be a real learning experience as well. It suddenly brought back long-forgotten, and perhaps repressed, memories of my childhood on my first day in Grade Six when I was surrounded by throngs of boisterous, clamoring students – except that now I was the teacher. Back on the farm, pesky mosquitoes could be swatted away – but here I was dealing with young children. Fortunately, as time progressed, I got used to this and began to greet each day with more confidence and self-assurance.

Over the years as a teacher in rural areas, I often met children who appeared to have been sharing a similar lifestyle I had experienced growing up on the farm. They were these more reclusive students, dressed a bit differently – maybe even smelling a bit differently, as well – and not appearing to be overly interested in books. They were, although, a bit slower or reluctant to react, generally very polite and always ready to lend a helping hand as long as it was not directly related to class work – something like hanging pictures and other paraphernalia on the walls. These students, I could easily relate to and, in a way, felt a bit of apprehension for them. I wondered what their first steps on their own in the outside world would be like. Would they falter and be unable to pick themselves up forcing them back to the familiar life on the farm or would they just unceremoniously dust themselves off and casually move on?

On the other hand, I would also meet their exact opposites – those kids who seemed to have it all, the Teflon kids, I would secretly call them. It was as if, for them, going through the rigors life was anything but a challenge and they could easily slide from one situation to another with apparent ease. They were gregarious, talkative and had a special verve for life. In other words, they were true social animals. Their main purpose seemed to be to enjoy life to its fullest without being bogged down or concerned with the drudgery of toiling daily just to keep bread on the table, as it were. Although most of them were equally polite, as far as kids go, they were definitely more outgoing, effervescent and even, I dare say, more obnoxious – not bad, just more difficult to deal with. These were the kids, however, who would probably be tomorrow's leaders and they were presumably just now learning the tricks of the trade, testing the waters, so to speak.

Then there were those who never really fitted in either camp – or perhaps fitted equally well in both. They could not be readily pigeon-holed, as it were, and would move fluidly – and perhaps aimlessly – from one camp to another not really seeming to be aware or caring what one group thought of the other. These students, by the way, were generally those picked by teachers to be monitors or go-betweens for their seemingly uncanny ability to defuse tense situations among their peers. Yes, I was still learning a lot about life even during these years.

But even while teaching, I would still sometimes reminisce about life on the farm – the good times as well as the bad. It seemed that even in the relative sanctuary of my own classroom, I still could not shed the trappings of my past. But then, I thought why would I want or need to? One does not choose his past. It was during these absent-minded moments that I would stop and wonder about what I would now be doing had I chosen to pursue life on the farm. Would I still be struggling with the elements and the soil or would I have left that piece of land and moved on to a more productive area and become a success as I know some of my childhood acquaintances had done? Would I have been able to avoid the perils and pitfalls experienced by my own parents and follow a road which would gradually have led me to a brighter future? These and many other questions often plagued me over the years. I guess the road never taken, as the poet Robert Frost had shown, will never be known in this lifetime. My own father, as well, who, I know, had once in his youth, entertained thoughts of becoming a barber before moving eastward to settle on a farm, had likewise taken a different road and ventured in a whole new direction. Perhaps, as another saying goes: the sins of the father …

In the end, though, no one in the family ever regretted making the move as each has become highly successful and is now set in his or her new lifestyle. Actually, most of us are now retired or semi-retired from the daily grind of working to earn a living and are now gradually sailing into that sunset of our lives armed with the memories of the past – a past, though, which, in the span of one lifetime, seems to have encompassed many generations. Hopefully, our own children will reap the benefits of our collective labors.

Chapter 15 – Epilogue

You wouldn't think that poverty
Could teach you anything,
That drought and wind and empty fields
Could make a fellow sing.
But I have learned that life holds more
Than all I ever knew,
The deep abiding lovely things
That live and stay with you.
Adapted from Hard Times
By Edna Jaques

My purpose in telling my story was not merely to chronicle the life of one family – mine – as it feverishly and religiously endeavored to deal with the overwhelming forces of nature pitted against it in what was then a very precarious and unfriendly environment. Rather, it was an attempt to bring these struggles to the forefront for all to see as well as to demonstrate the temper of the times shared by countless rural families in the post-Depression era in the Canadian West. It is often noted that the Depression period was one of incomparable and unmitigated disasters and countless hardships which have yet to be replicated, either in the past or in the present. However, it is often forgotten that the period which immediately followed it was equally harsh on a disproportionally large number of people whose lives have been irrevocably affected by the endless struggles they had to contend with, and, unfortunately for me, my family was included.

If I have succeeded, even in a miniscule way, to make people reminisce and take notice of the many hardships and misfortunes endured by those living then – and hopefully, by extension, those living now – perhaps even the world over, I will gladly consider it my humble contribution to bringing to light the burdens borne by these unfortunate souls of this world. In a world in which some people have so much, it is sometimes easy to forget that many more were – and still are – living dangerously near the edge of a taunting precipice which threatens, at any moment, to engulf them in its cavernous maw.

Of course, many books have been written about the lives of the poor, as well as the dispossessed, and by much better story-tellers or chroniclers than I could ever hope to be. However, until and unless one has, or has had, personal and authentic experience in that world, it is often difficult to relate realistically to these lifestyles. It is one thing to write about them but it is quite another to have directly lived through them. I am not sad or sorry for the difficult times my family and I went through, since growing up as we have, at least, not only brought us closer together but also made us all stronger and better able to withstand the rigors of daily life. The past, no matter how difficult, always has important lessons to teach us. And, mine and my family's was no different. Of course, we have missed out on a lot because of this lifestyle. It has, however, made us more aware of the plight of the disenfranchised and poverty-stricken, not only in our own backyard but in the rest of the world as well. Can one truly believe that the Donald Trumps and the Bernie Madoffs of this world are, in any sense, capable of genuinely empathizing with the downtrodden of this world?

Furthermore, I feel that my own childhood has been a sort of testimony for the very real need for governments – and private individuals – to try with ever greater resolve to help and support not only their own impoverished people but also those of other nations as well. And to repeat what I previously noted, needless to say, many people in our situation at the time would certainly have welcomed such help. Unfortunately, it was never forthcoming. Under the skin, we are all brethrens and nothing drives that fact home more than shared hard times. It may not be necessary to experience destitution directly before one is persuaded to do what one can do to try to alleviate the burdens of those who have so little, but it certainly brings such issues into better focus and goes a long way in providing a deeper, if nothing else, understanding of those issues. You just can't play hockey from the comfort of your living room. Today, while reflecting on my past, I am truly thankful for having broken this cycle of poverty in my little corner of the world – even if it came at a price, that of turning away from this past. My life has improved tremendously since the days of toiling in those distant sand-covered fields under a torrid midday sun so many years ago.

And yet, it should also, in all fairness, be vigorously pointed out that even the meagerness of my own childhood pales abysmally in comparison with the dismal and abject poverty experienced by countless millions the world over, even in our own midst. It is one area where we can't afford to be smug. It is incumbent on all of us to face these too real and highly visible – thanks to the advent of television sets in our living rooms – challenges and facts of life squarely and not shy away from them. Each one of us, in fact, has an inalienable right and sacred duty to help publicize the plight of unfortunate people the world over and try to bring the full weights of governments to bear on their misfortunes – hence the main reason for this expose.

It certainly boggles the mind to think of all the personal stories and tragedies out there which have yet to be written about each of the millions who succumb every day to the rigors of daily life. Only by elevating their plight to the forefront, can we hope to alleviate their misery. It is a well-documented, albeit very disturbing, fact that there are now proportionally more people living in squalid conditions then there were a generation or so ago in spite of the development of new technologies. Perhaps, I might even tread softly here and venture to say that governments – enlightened governments, that is – should probably have access to some of that wealth in order to help the plight of the most unfortunate of their citizens. But this, considering the rampant accumulation of ill-gotten wealth by those in power, I fear, is only dreaming in Technicolor, as it were, and at best, perhaps only a whimper in the dark, by one who has been there and is glad to have crossed his Rubicon. Yet, there is still hope on the horizon as some rays of sunlight appear to have begun to pierce this veil of darkness. But then, as usual, I digress.

Farms, as well, for the most part, nowadays have also grown enormously large and prosperous. Gone, also, for the most part, is the little struggling family farm – like the friendly little corner grocery store – except for the few remaining ones still trying to hang on to their nostalgic past. But even these are rapidly being absorbed by these fast-growing conglomerates. Our own farm, as well, where we had entertained dreams – now completely shattered - of turning into an oasis of plenty was doomed at the end, like many others, to follow a path toward obsolescence and become part of a larger entity.

In fact, farming has now become only one facet of what has now become agribusinesses as many of them are wholly or partly owned by business concerns whose sole raison d'etre has become the accumulation of wealth for its own sake. That, of itself, may not be altogether bad. They are not anymore, however, the focal point, of the rich social and cultural life they once were in the past. In fact, they now appear to be circumnavigating uneasily on the periphery of society – like some huge awkward lumbering behemoths – as if ashamed to have relinquished their social responsibilities for more material rewards. While some might be tempted to disparage at such developments, even lament the passing away of the small family farms, and perhaps with good reason, this alternative to these vast enterprises, although it might sound appealing, even romantic, is not one that I would particularly like to revisit. Just as the business community arguably fares better with large conglomerates, so does the farming sector.

Perhaps, in a convoluted sense, it is the only way the small family farm can finally be rescued from an unmerciful demise and perhaps also, in a strange way, help to eradicate still-existent pockets of poverty in the countryside. Granted, these large entities are not doing it out of the goodness of their own hearts but sometimes, maybe, just maybe, the end justifies the means. The challenge is for everyone to try to foster a sense of social conscience in large corporations to make it their primary role to look after those struggling few who, in fact, enable these concerns to endure in our midst.

If being raised in poverty has taught me one thing, it is that it can, nay must, be addressed by the world community if everyone is to participate fully in that world. What does it benefit our world if many of its citizens are abandoned on its fringes to linger in squalor while the rest moves forward and enjoys the fruits of this world? As humans, should we not all endeavor to bring everyone into the fold, as it were, and ensure at least a semblance of equal justice and participation to all. Live on the edge for a while then tell the world that life is just fine there. I doubt that many people would want to do that. And just as you would want to extricate yourself from such a situation, so would everyone else. All they need is some help and direction. This is where each and every one of us comes in. So let us move forward and not repeat the mistakes of our past. This is my challenge for future generations. Will they be up to it? Only time will tell.

About the author

Ron Nicolas was born and raised in Southeastern Manitoba, Canada. He received his Bachelor of Arts, Master of Arts and Bachelor of Education degrees from the University of Manitoba and spent most of his adult life teaching in the Public Schools System. He is the author of 'Northern Lights – A Wilderness Adventure' – a fictional account based on his own experiences in Manitoba's North. He is presently working on a third novel which will form a sequel to Northern Lights. He now resides in Winnipeg, Manitoba with his family.